The Stories of Great Rulers

Shah Rukh

Published by Shah Rukh, 2024.

THE STORIES OF GREAT RULERS

First edition. May 28, 2024.

Copyright © 2024 Shah Rukh.

ISBN: 979-8224931637

Written by Shah Rukh.

Table of Contents

Prologue

In the annals of history, there are figures whose names echo through the corridors of time, their deeds and legacies shaping the course of nations and civilizations. They are the Great Rulers, men and women of vision, courage, and ambition, whose stories captivate our imaginations and inspire awe and admiration.

"The Stories of Great Rulers" is a journey through the lives and reigns of these remarkable individuals, spanning centuries and continents, from the banks of the Nile to the shores of distant lands. In these pages, we delve into the triumphs and tribulations of monarchs and emperors, queens and empresses, whose destinies were intertwined with the fate of their people and their realms.

From the legendary pharaohs of ancient Egypt to the mighty conquerors of the ancient world, from the enlightened monarchs of the Renaissance to the powerful emperors of the modern era, each chapter of this book unveils the epic saga of a ruler who left an indelible mark on history.

But beyond the grandeur of their palaces and the glory of their conquests, we discover the human faces behind the crowns—their hopes and fears, their loves and losses, their triumphs and tragedies. We witness their struggles against adversity, their quests for power and prestige, and their efforts to leave a lasting legacy for generations to come.

As we journey through the lives of these Great Rulers, we are reminded of the timeless lessons they impart—the importance of leadership and statesmanship, the consequences of ambition and hubris, and the enduring power of courage, compassion, and wisdom.

Join us now as we embark on an unforgettable odyssey through the corridors of power and the pages of history, guided by the stories of the Great Rulers who shaped the world in which we live.

Chapter 1: Hammurabi of Babylon

Hammurabi, born around 1810 BCE, was the sixth king of the First Babylonian Dynasty, reigning from approximately 1792 BCE until his death in 1750 BCE. His reign is often regarded as a pivotal period in ancient Mesopotamian history due to his significant contributions to law, administration, and empire-building. Hammurabi's impact extended far beyond his lifetime, influencing legal systems and governance structures for millennia.

Hammurabi ascended the throne of Babylon, a city-state in central Mesopotamia, during a time of considerable political fragmentation. The region was divided among various city-states, each vying for dominance. Hammurabi inherited a kingdom that was relatively small compared to its neighbors, such as Larsa, Eshnunna, and the more distant Elam. His early reign was marked by strategic diplomacy and alliances, as he carefully consolidated power and built a robust administrative apparatus.

One of Hammurabi's most notable achievements was the codification of laws, now famously known as the Code of Hammurabi. This comprehensive set of laws, inscribed on a stele, covered various aspects of daily life, including trade, marriage, property rights, and criminal justice. The code is often celebrated for its early attempt to establish a legal framework based on justice and equity, encapsulated in the principle of "an eye for an eye." However, it is essential to note that the code also reflected the hierarchical and patriarchal nature of Babylonian society, with different punishments prescribed for different social classes and genders.

Hammurabi's legal code was revolutionary in its methodical approach to justice and governance. It served as a public declaration of the king's commitment to maintaining order and protecting his subjects. The stele bearing the code was placed in a public location, likely a temple, to ensure that it was accessible to the populace. This transparency was a significant step forward in the administration of justice, as it provided a clear and consistent set of expectations for behavior and legal consequences.

In addition to his legal reforms, Hammurabi was a skilled military strategist and tactician. He gradually expanded his territory through a combination of diplomacy, warfare, and strategic marriages. Early in his reign, he focused on strengthening Babylon's economic and military resources. He built canals, improved agricultural productivity, and fortified cities. These efforts not only enhanced the kingdom's prosperity but also its capacity to wage war effectively.

Hammurabi's military campaigns were often calculated and opportunistic. He capitalized on the internal strife and weaknesses of neighboring states. One of his key military achievements was the defeat of Rim-Sin of Larsa, a formidable rival who had controlled much of southern Mesopotamia. By conquering Larsa, Hammurabi gained control over vital trade routes and fertile lands, significantly enhancing Babylon's economic power.

The conquest of Larsa marked the beginning of Hammurabi's transformation from a regional ruler to an empire builder. Over the next few decades, he continued to expand his domain, incorporating cities such as Eshnunna, Mari, and Assyria into his empire. His campaigns extended Babylonian influence across much of Mesopotamia, creating one of the largest and most powerful empires of the ancient Near East.

Hammurabi's success as a ruler was not solely due to his military prowess. He was also an adept administrator who understood the importance of effective governance. He centralized administrative functions, appointing loyal officials to key positions and ensuring that his decrees were enforced throughout his realm. He also undertook extensive building projects, constructing temples, walls, and other public works that enhanced both the infrastructure and the cultural prestige of his empire.

One of the enduring legacies of Hammurabi's reign was the integration of diverse cultures and peoples within his empire. Mesopotamia was a region of great ethnic and cultural diversity, and Hammurabi's ability to govern such a varied population was a testament to his administrative skills. He allowed a degree of local autonomy, respecting existing traditions and customs, while simultaneously promoting a cohesive legal and administrative framework.

Hammurabi's reign also saw significant developments in religion and culture. He was a devout worshipper of Marduk, the chief deity of Babylon, and he played a crucial role in elevating Marduk's status within the Mesopotamian pantheon. Under Hammurabi's rule, Babylon became a major religious center, attracting pilgrims and scholars from across the region. This religious centralization further solidified Hammurabi's authority and the unity of his empire.

Despite his many accomplishments, Hammurabi's empire began to decline towards the end of his reign and after his death. The vast territories he had conquered proved difficult to manage, and internal revolts, as well as external pressures, gradually eroded Babylonian dominance. Nevertheless, Hammurabi's legacy endured through his legal code and the administrative precedents he set.

The Code of Hammurabi remains one of the most significant artifacts of ancient legal history. It provides invaluable insights into the social, economic, and legal practices of ancient Mesopotamia. The principles enshrined in the code influenced subsequent legal systems in the Near East and beyond, echoing through the ages as a foundational element of the rule of law.

Hammurabi's ability to balance military conquest with legal and administrative reforms established a model for future rulers. His reign exemplified the potential for a strong, centralized state to bring order and prosperity to a diverse and often fractious region. His emphasis on justice, infrastructure, and religious patronage set standards that would inspire later generations of leaders.

Chapter 2: Queen Hatshepsut of Egypt

Queen Hatshepsut, born around 1508 BCE, was one of ancient Egypt's most successful and fascinating rulers, reigning from approximately 1479 to 1458 BCE. As the fifth pharaoh of the Eighteenth Dynasty, she is renowned for her unprecedented ascent to power as a female king, her extensive building projects, and her prosperous reign which marked a period of great wealth and artistic achievement for Egypt. Hatshepsut's story is unique not only for her achievements but also for the gender dynamics and political intrigue that characterized her reign.

Hatshepsut was born into the royal family, the daughter of Pharaoh Thutmose I and his queen, Ahmose. Her name, which means "Foremost of Noble Ladies," reflected her high status. As was customary in the royal family, she married her half-brother Thutmose II, solidifying her position within the ruling elite. Thutmose II's reign was relatively short and uneventful, and upon his death, the throne passed to his son by a secondary wife, Thutmose III. At this time, Thutmose III was still a child, and Hatshepsut assumed the role of regent, ostensibly to guide the young king until he came of age.

Hatshepsut's regency, however, quickly evolved into something far more significant. Within a few years, she took the unprecedented step of declaring herself pharaoh, adopting full royal titulary and the regalia of kingship. This included donning the false beard traditionally worn by male pharaohs and being depicted in the masculine form in statues and reliefs. This bold move was justified through a combination of religious and political strategies. Hatshepsut claimed divine sanction for her rule, presenting herself as the chosen of the god Amun and emphasizing her divine birth, wherein Amun himself was said to have fathered her.

Despite these measures, Hatshepsut's assumption of power was not merely an act of self-aggrandizement. She proved to be an extraordinarily effective ruler, overseeing a period of internal stability, economic prosperity, and extensive architectural achievements. One of her most significant contributions was her ambitious building program, which included the construction of her magnificent mortuary temple at Deir el-Bahri. This temple, nestled in the cliffs of the Theban Necropolis, is considered one of the architectural marvels of ancient Egypt. Its design, characterized by terraces, colonnades, and detailed reliefs, reflects both the grandeur and sophistication of Hatshepsut's reign.

In addition to her mortuary temple, Hatshepsut commissioned numerous other projects, including the erection of obelisks at Karnak, the construction of temples and chapels throughout Egypt, and the restoration of monuments damaged during previous reigns. These projects not only demonstrated her piety and devotion to the gods but also served to legitimize her rule and cement her legacy. The high quality and artistic excellence of the works commissioned during her reign speak to a flourishing of artistic and architectural endeavors.

Hatshepsut's reign was also marked by successful foreign policy and trade expeditions. One of the most famous of these was the expedition to the Land of Punt, an exotic and mysterious realm likely located along the coast of the Horn of Africa. The expedition, which is extensively documented in the reliefs at Deir el-Bahri, brought back a wealth of goods, including myrrh, frankincense, gold, ivory, and exotic animals. These trade missions not only enriched Egypt but also showcased Hatshepsut's ability to project power and influence beyond the traditional borders of the kingdom.

Despite her many achievements, Hatshepsut's reign was not without its challenges. The fact that she was a female pharaoh in a traditionally male role undoubtedly posed difficulties. However, she navigated these challenges with skill and pragmatism, often portraying herself in masculine terms while simultaneously emphasizing her unique position as a woman chosen by the gods. Her co-regency with

Thutmose III, who was technically the rightful king, required careful management to maintain stability and prevent potential power struggles.

The end of Hatshepsut's reign remains somewhat mysterious. It is believed that she died around 1458 BCE, but the circumstances of her death are not well-documented. Following her death, Thutmose III became the sole ruler and embarked on a campaign to erase Hatshepsut's legacy. Statues were defaced, inscriptions were chiseled away, and her name was omitted from official king lists. This act of damnatio memoriae, or condemnation of memory, was likely an attempt by Thutmose III to reassert traditional gender norms and solidify his own legacy.

However, despite these efforts to erase her from history, Hatshepsut's legacy has endured. Modern archaeological discoveries and research have gradually restored her to her rightful place as one of Egypt's greatest pharaohs. Her mortuary temple at Deir el-Bahri stands as a testament to her architectural vision and the prosperity of her reign. The story of her rise to power, her achievements, and her eventual erasure offers a fascinating glimpse into the complexities of ancient Egyptian politics, gender roles, and religious practices.

Hatshepsut's reign is also significant for its broader implications on the role of women in leadership. While ancient Egypt did have other female rulers, Hatshepsut's successful and prosperous reign challenged traditional gender norms and demonstrated the potential for female leadership in a male-dominated society. Her ability to command respect and maintain stability while undertaking ambitious projects and successful foreign expeditions is a testament to her political acumen and administrative skill.

Chapter 3: King Tutankhamun of Egypt

King Tutankhamun, often referred to as King Tut, reigned during one of the most tumultuous and intriguing periods in ancient Egyptian history. Born around 1341 BCE, Tutankhamun ascended to the throne at a very young age and ruled until his premature death at approximately 18 or 19 years old, around 1323 BCE. Despite his relatively short reign, Tutankhamun's life and legacy have captivated historians and the public alike, particularly after the discovery of his nearly intact tomb in 1922 by British archaeologist Howard Carter. This discovery provided an unprecedented glimpse into the wealth, art, and burial practices of ancient Egypt, making Tutankhamun one of the most famous pharaohs.

Tutankhamun was born during the late Eighteenth Dynasty, a period marked by significant religious and political upheaval. His father, Akhenaten, was a revolutionary pharaoh who established the worship of the Aten, the sun disk, as the primary religion, in what is often referred to as the Amarna Period. Akhenaten's radical monotheism, which involved the suppression of the traditional polytheistic cults, particularly that of Amun, caused substantial disruption in Egyptian society. The capital was moved from Thebes to a new city, Akhetaten (modern-day Amarna), dedicated to the Aten. This shift not only disrupted the religious structure but also the administrative and economic systems, causing widespread dissatisfaction.

Tutankhamun was originally named Tutankhaten, reflecting his father's devotion to the Aten. However, after Akhenaten's death, there was a concerted effort to restore the traditional religious practices and the worship of Amun. This restoration effort was overseen by powerful figures such as Ay, who was likely a high-ranking official and advisor, and Horemheb, a military general. These advisors played crucial roles in guiding the young king and ensuring the stability of the kingdom during this period of transition.

Around the age of nine, Tutankhaten ascended the throne, and shortly thereafter, his name was changed to Tutankhamun, signaling a return to the worship of Amun. His reign saw the dismantling of his father's religious reforms and the restoration of the traditional gods and temples. The capital was moved back to Thebes, and efforts were made to rebuild and repair the temples that had been neglected or damaged during Akhenaten's rule. This period of restoration was essential in re-establishing the socio-religious balance in Egypt.

Despite his young age, Tutankhamun's reign was marked by significant administrative and religious reforms aimed at stabilizing the country. Edicts were issued to restore the priesthoods and their associated lands and wealth, and extensive building projects were undertaken to reaffirm the glory of the Amun cult and other traditional deities. The king's image and cartouches were prominently displayed in these temples, reinforcing his legitimacy and divine favor.

One of the most intriguing aspects of Tutankhamun's reign is his personal life, which has been pieced together through various archaeological findings. He was married to Ankhesenamun, who was likely his half-sister and a daughter of Akhenaten and Nefertiti. This marriage was probably intended to solidify the royal lineage and reinforce the continuity of the ruling family. Despite their efforts, the couple did not produce a surviving heir. The mummified remains of two stillborn daughters were found in Tutankhamun's tomb, underscoring the personal tragedies that befell the young king.

Tutankhamun's health has been a subject of considerable debate among scholars. Analysis of his mummy and other archaeological evidence suggests that he suffered from several health issues, including a cleft palate, a clubfoot, and possibly a form of temporal lobe epilepsy. DNA studies have also revealed that he had multiple malarial infections, which could have contributed to his early death. These findings suggest that the royal family might have been plagued by genetic disorders due to the practice of intermarriage.

The cause of Tutankhamun's death has been a topic of speculation and investigation. Early theories ranged from murder to an accident. A detailed analysis of his mummy revealed a fracture in his left thighbone, leading some to speculate that he might have died from an infection resulting from a broken leg. More recent studies suggest that his death was likely the result of complications from multiple health problems, exacerbated by a severe malarial infection.

Tutankhamun's death marked the end of an era, and the throne passed to his advisor Ay, followed by the military leader Horemheb. Both rulers continued the efforts to erase the memory of the Amarna Period and restore traditional religious practices. Tutankhamun's contributions were overshadowed by his successors' more aggressive campaigns to re-establish the status quo.

The most significant event that brought Tutankhamun to global prominence occurred millennia after his death. In 1922, Howard Carter discovered his tomb in the Valley of the Kings. This tomb, designated KV62, was remarkable for its relatively undisturbed state and the wealth of artifacts it contained. The discovery included a vast array of treasures: gold coffins, a golden funerary mask, chariots, thrones, and a wealth of other items intended to accompany the king into the afterlife. The opulence of these grave goods provided unprecedented insight into the burial practices and material culture of ancient Egypt's elite.

The discovery of Tutankhamun's tomb had a profound impact on both Egyptology and popular culture. The wealth and beauty of the artifacts captivated the world and sparked a renewed interest in ancient Egypt. The "Tut-mania" that followed influenced art, fashion, and literature, and established Tutankhamun as one of the most iconic figures of ancient history.

Despite the fame brought by his tomb, Tutankhamun himself remains an enigmatic figure. His reign, though relatively short, played a crucial role in the transition from the Amarna Period back to traditional Egyptian religious and cultural practices. His efforts to restore the old gods and repair the temples damaged during his father's rule were significant in re-establishing stability in a time of considerable upheaval.

The enduring fascination with Tutankhamun lies in the combination of his dramatic life story, the mystery surrounding his death, and the unparalleled archaeological treasures found in his tomb. His golden mask, with its serene and youthful visage, has become one of the most recognizable symbols of ancient Egypt. The artifacts from his tomb continue to be studied, revealing new insights into the art, technology, and daily life of ancient Egyptians.

Chapter 4: Queen Nefertiti of Egypt

Queen Nefertiti, who lived circa 1370–1330 BCE, remains one of the most enigmatic and captivating figures in ancient Egyptian history. As the Great Royal Wife of Pharaoh Akhenaten, she played a pivotal role in one of the most revolutionary periods of ancient Egypt, known as the Amarna Period. Nefertiti's legacy extends far beyond her beauty, famously captured in the iconic bust now housed in the Neues Museum in Berlin. Her life and influence encompassed profound religious and cultural changes, and her story continues to fascinate historians, archaeologists, and the public alike.

Nefertiti's origins are somewhat obscure, though she is believed to have been born around 1370 BCE. Some theories suggest she was the daughter of Ay, who later became pharaoh, and his wife Tey, making her a native Egyptian. Other theories propose that she might have been a foreign princess, possibly from Mitanni, an ancient kingdom in northern Syria. Regardless of her origins, Nefertiti rose to prominence through her marriage to Amenhotep IV, who later took the name Akhenaten.

Nefertiti married Akhenaten around 1352 BCE, and the couple had six daughters: Meritaten, Meketaten, Ankhesenpaaten (later known as Ankhesenamun), Neferneferuaten Tasherit, Neferneferure, and Setepenre. The prominence of her daughters in various inscriptions and reliefs suggests that Nefertiti had a significant influence in the royal court and possibly a powerful role in state affairs. As queen, she was depicted in an unprecedented manner, often shown participating in religious rituals and depicted with the same scale and prominence as the pharaoh.

The most revolutionary aspect of Nefertiti and Akhenaten's reign was the religious transformation they spearheaded. Akhenaten shifted the religious focus from the traditional pantheon of gods, centered around Amun, to the worship of the Aten, the sun disk. This religious revolution, often referred to as the Amarna Revolution, established a form of monotheism or henotheism, with the Aten as the supreme deity. This change was not merely religious but also political, as it reduced the power of the traditional priesthood, particularly the priests of Amun, and centralized religious authority under the pharaoh and his family.

Nefertiti was a central figure in this new religious order. She was often depicted alongside Akhenaten in worship scenes, participating actively in the rituals dedicated to the Aten. This portrayal was highly unusual for a queen, indicating her unique status and the possible co-regency with Akhenaten. The famous limestone bust of Nefertiti, discovered in the workshop of the sculptor Thutmose, reflects her elevated status and the artistic innovation of the Amarna Period. The bust is renowned for its exquisite craftsmanship and the striking depiction of Nefertiti's beauty.

The couple's relocation of the capital to Akhetaten (modern-day Amarna) symbolized their commitment to the Aten. This new city was built rapidly and featured distinctive art and architecture that broke away from traditional styles. The art of the Amarna Period is characterized by a sense of realism and intimacy, with depictions of the royal family in affectionate poses, a significant departure from the formal and idealized representations typical of earlier periods.

Despite the initial success of Akhenaten and Nefertiti's religious reforms, their reign faced considerable challenges. The shift to Atenism disrupted the established religious, economic, and political systems. The traditional priesthood and the administrative class, which had vested interests in the old order, likely opposed these changes. Furthermore, the new capital, Akhetaten, isolated the pharaoh from the administrative heart of Egypt, leading to possible neglect of state affairs.

Nefertiti's role in the later years of Akhenaten's reign and her fate after his death remain subjects of considerable speculation. Some scholars believe that she may have continued to rule as a co-regent or even as a pharaoh in her own right under the name Neferneferuaten. This theory is supported by inscriptions and artifacts that suggest a female pharaoh who co-ruled or succeeded Akhenaten. However, this identification is debated, and alternative theories propose that this ruler could have been their daughter Meritaten or another royal woman.

The decline of the Amarna Period began with the death of Akhenaten around 1336 BCE. The subsequent rulers, including Smenkhkare, Tutankhaten (later Tutankhamun), and Ay, sought to restore the traditional religious practices and return to Thebes. This restoration involved dismantling Akhenaten's religious reforms, abandoning Akhetaten, and reinstating the worship of Amun and the traditional gods. The art and monuments of the Amarna Period were defaced, and attempts were made to erase the memory of Akhenaten and his immediate successors from the historical record.

The discovery of Nefertiti's bust by German archaeologist Ludwig Borchardt in 1912 brought her international fame and highlighted the artistic achievements of the Amarna Period. The bust, with its serene beauty and strikingly modern aesthetic, has become one of the most iconic images of ancient Egypt. It symbolizes both the artistic innovation of the Amarna Period and the enigmatic allure of Nefertiti herself.

Recent archaeological discoveries and technological advances have continued to shed light on Nefertiti's life and reign. Excavations at Amarna, DNA analysis of mummies, and new interpretations of inscriptions have provided insights into her role and the broader context of the period. However, the ultimate fate of Nefertiti remains elusive. Her tomb has not been conclusively identified, although some researchers believe she may be buried in a hidden chamber within or near Tutankhamun's tomb, based on radar scans and other evidence.

Nefertiti's legacy endures not only through her contributions to the religious and cultural landscape of ancient Egypt but also through the ongoing fascination with her life and times. She represents a powerful and dynamic figure in a period of significant transformation and upheaval. Her story, intertwined with that of Akhenaten and the Amarna Period, offers valuable insights into the complexities of ancient Egyptian politics, religion, and society.

Chapter 5: King David of Israel

King David of Israel, who reigned approximately from 1010 to 970 BCE, is one of the most significant and multifaceted figures in the history of the ancient Near East. His life and legacy have been chronicled in the Hebrew Bible, particularly in the books of Samuel, Kings, and Chronicles, and his influence extends into the religious, cultural, and political spheres of Judaism, Christianity, and Islam. David's story encompasses his rise from a shepherd boy to the founding monarch of a unified Israelite kingdom, his military conquests, his personal flaws and tribulations, and his lasting impact on religious traditions and cultural heritage.

David's early life is portrayed in the biblical narrative as humble and unassuming. He was the youngest son of Jesse, a resident of Bethlehem in the territory of Judah. David's initial anointing by the prophet Samuel, as described in 1 Samuel 16, marked the beginning of his journey from obscurity to prominence. Samuel was directed by God to anoint David as the future king of Israel, despite Saul still being the reigning monarch. This divine selection underscored a central theme in David's story: his role as the chosen one, blessed by God with a special destiny.

David first gained national attention through his encounter with Goliath, the Philistine giant. According to the biblical account in 1 Samuel 17, young David, armed with only a sling and stones, defeated Goliath, showcasing his courage, faith, and divine favor. This victory was not only a turning point for David personally but also for the Israelite nation, as it shifted the momentum in their ongoing conflict with the Philistines. David's triumph over Goliath became emblematic of the underdog prevailing through faith and bravery, a narrative that resonates deeply within the collective cultural memory of Western civilization.

Following his victory, David entered the service of King Saul. Initially, he served as a musician, playing the harp to soothe Saul's troubled spirit. However, David's military prowess soon became apparent, and he rose through the ranks to become a successful commander. His close friendship with Saul's son Jonathan and his marriage to Saul's daughter Michal further integrated him into the royal household. Despite these connections, Saul grew increasingly jealous of David's popularity and military success, viewing him as a threat to his throne.

Saul's jealousy and paranoia culminated in multiple attempts on David's life, forcing David to flee and live as a fugitive. During this period, David assembled a loyal band of followers and built a reputation as a formidable leader and tactician. His time in exile was marked by a series of skirmishes with Saul's forces and strategic alliances, including with the Philistines at times, highlighting his survival skills and political acumen. These experiences in the wilderness forged David's leadership qualities and deepened his reliance on divine guidance.

The turning point came with the deaths of Saul and Jonathan in a battle against the Philistines on Mount Gilboa. With Saul's demise, David was anointed king over the tribe of Judah in Hebron, while Saul's son Ish-bosheth briefly ruled over the northern tribes. After a protracted civil war and Ish-bosheth's assassination, David became the undisputed king of a unified Israel around 1003 BCE. His consolidation of power marked the beginning of the United Monarchy, a period of political unification and territorial expansion for the Israelite nation.

David's reign as king was characterized by significant military conquests and administrative achievements. He established Jerusalem as the political and spiritual capital of Israel, capturing the city from the Jebusites and bringing the Ark of the Covenant there, symbolizing the centralization of religious worship. Jerusalem, often referred to as the "City of David," became the enduring center of Jewish religious and national identity. David's military campaigns extended Israel's borders, subduing neighboring enemies such as the Philistines, Moabites, Ammonites, Edomites, and Arameans. These victories secured Israel's dominance in the region and established David's reputation as a mighty warrior king.

Despite his military and political successes, David's reign was not without controversy and personal failures. One of the most well-known episodes in David's life is his affair with Bathsheba, the wife of Uriah the Hittite. As recounted in 2 Samuel 11, David's desire for Bathsheba led him to orchestrate Uriah's death in battle, an act that brought severe condemnation from the prophet Nathan. Nathan's rebuke, and the subsequent turmoil within David's family, highlighted the moral complexities and human flaws of the king. This incident and its aftermath, including the rebellion of his son Absalom, underscored the themes of repentance, divine justice, and the consequences of personal sin.

David's later years were marked by efforts to secure his legacy and prepare for the succession of his kingdom. He faced further internal strife, including the revolt of his son Adonijah, but ultimately ensured that his son Solomon would succeed him. David's instructions to Solomon, recorded in 1 Kings 2, reflected his desire for a stable and prosperous kingdom governed by adherence to divine law.

David's death around 970 BCE marked the end of an era, but his legacy endured in various forms. Solomon's reign, characterized by wisdom, wealth, and the construction of the First Temple in Jerusalem, was seen as the fulfillment of David's vision for Israel. The Davidic dynasty continued to rule Judah for centuries, and the promise of an eternal dynasty, as articulated in the Davidic Covenant, became a cornerstone of Jewish messianic expectations.

Beyond his political and military achievements, David's cultural and religious contributions were profound. He is traditionally credited with composing many of the Psalms, which are central to Jewish and Christian liturgies. The Psalms attributed to David express a wide range of emotions and themes, from profound lament and penitence to jubilant praise and thanksgiving, reflecting his deep spiritual life and relationship with God. These poetic and musical compositions have had a lasting impact on religious worship and devotional practices.

David's legacy extends into the religious traditions of Judaism, Christianity, and Islam. In Judaism, he is remembered as the ideal king, a symbol of the messianic hope for the restoration of the Davidic line and the establishment of a just and peaceful kingdom. Christianity views David as a precursor to Jesus Christ, who is often referred to as the "Son of David" and seen as the fulfillment of the messianic prophecies associated with the Davidic line. In Islam, David (Dawud) is revered as a prophet and a king, known for his piety, wisdom, and contributions to religious law and poetry.

In addition to religious texts, David's life and reign have inspired countless works of art, literature, and music throughout history. From Michelangelo's famous statue of David to Handel's oratorio "Saul," his story has been retold and reinterpreted in various cultural contexts. These artistic representations often emphasize different aspects of David's character and legacy, from his youthful bravery and divine favor to his moral struggles and repentance.

The historical accuracy of the biblical accounts of David's life has been a topic of scholarly debate. While the archaeological evidence for David's reign is limited, discoveries such as the Tel Dan Stele, which references the "House of David," provide some corroboration of his historical existence. Scholars continue to examine the biblical narrative critically, considering both its theological significance and its potential historical basis.

Chapter 6: King Solomon of Israel

King Solomon of Israel, who reigned from approximately 970 to 931 BCE, is one of the most renowned figures in the annals of ancient history. Solomon's rule is often regarded as the golden age of Israel, characterized by unprecedented prosperity, extensive building projects, and a reputation for unparalleled wisdom. As the son of King David and Bathsheba, Solomon inherited a unified and expanding kingdom and further cemented the legacy of the Davidic dynasty. His story, which is primarily detailed in the Hebrew Bible's books of Kings and Chronicles, as well as other religious texts, has left a lasting impact on the cultural, religious, and historical landscapes of Judaism, Christianity, and Islam.

Solomon's ascent to the throne was marked by political intrigue and familial conflict. As David's health declined, a power struggle ensued among his sons. Adonijah, Solomon's older half-brother, declared himself king with the support of key figures, including Joab, the commander of David's army, and Abiathar, the priest. However, Bathsheba and the prophet Nathan, who were ardent supporters of Solomon, intervened to ensure David's promise that Solomon would succeed him. David's endorsement and the swift actions of Solomon's supporters led to his anointing as king, effectively quashing Adonijah's rebellion. This early demonstration of political acumen and decisive action set the tone for Solomon's reign.

Upon securing the throne, Solomon swiftly consolidated his power by eliminating potential rivals. He ordered the execution of Adonijah, Joab, and Shimei, and exiled Abiathar. These actions, while ruthless, were necessary to stabilize his rule and prevent future insurrections. Solomon's political astuteness in these early years laid the foundation for a reign marked by stability and prosperity.

One of the most defining aspects of Solomon's reign was his renowned wisdom. According to the biblical account in 1 Kings 3,

Solomon famously asked God for wisdom to govern his people justly, rather than requesting long life, wealth, or the death of his enemies. Pleased by Solomon's request, God granted him unparalleled wisdom, as well as riches and honor. Solomon's wisdom became legendary, attracting admirers and dignitaries from far and wide. The visit of the Queen of Sheba, as described in 1 Kings 10, is one of the most famous examples. She came to test Solomon with hard questions and was astounded by his insights and the splendor of his court. This visit not only underscored Solomon's intellectual prowess but also established diplomatic and economic ties between Israel and the distant kingdom of Sheba.

Solomon's wisdom was not confined to political and judicial matters; it also encompassed literary and scientific pursuits. He is traditionally credited with composing many of the Proverbs, Ecclesiastes, and the Song of Songs (Song of Solomon), which are part of the Hebrew Bible's wisdom literature. These writings reflect profound insights into human nature, morality, and the complexities of life. Proverbs, in particular, offers practical advice on ethical living and is still widely read and referenced for its timeless wisdom. Ecclesiastes delves into the existential search for meaning and the transient nature of worldly pursuits, while the Song of Songs celebrates romantic love and is often interpreted allegorically in religious traditions.

Solomon's reign was also distinguished by monumental building projects, the most famous of which was the construction of the First Temple in Jerusalem. This grand edifice, also known as Solomon's Temple, became the central place of worship for the Israelites and a symbol of their covenant with God. The detailed descriptions of the Temple's construction in 1 Kings 6-7 and 2 Chronicles 3-4 highlight its grandeur and the intricate craftsmanship involved. Solomon enlisted the help of Hiram, the king of Tyre, to supply cedar and cypress wood, as well as skilled laborers. The Temple's completion not only fulfilled

David's vision but also solidified Jerusalem's status as the spiritual and political heart of Israel.

The Temple served multiple functions: it was the primary location for religious rituals, including sacrifices and festivals, and it housed the Ark of the Covenant, which contained the tablets of the Ten Commandments. The dedication of the Temple, as described in 1 Kings 8, was a momentous occasion marked by elaborate ceremonies, prayers, and sacrifices. Solomon's dedicatory prayer emphasized the Temple as a place where God's presence would dwell and where the Israelites could seek forgiveness and guidance. This event underscored the centrality of the Temple in the religious life of Israel and its role as a tangible manifestation of the nation's covenant with God.

Beyond the Temple, Solomon undertook numerous other building projects that contributed to the kingdom's prosperity and infrastructure. He fortified key cities, constructed palaces, and developed a network of trade routes. The strategic location of Israel allowed Solomon to capitalize on the trade between Egypt, Arabia, and Mesopotamia. His extensive commercial enterprises included trade in precious metals, spices, and luxury goods, which brought immense wealth to the kingdom. The biblical account in 1 Kings 10:14-29 describes the vast wealth that flowed into Solomon's coffers, including gold, silver, ivory, and exotic animals. This wealth enabled Solomon to maintain a lavish court and fund his ambitious building programs.

Solomon's administrative reforms also played a crucial role in the prosperity of his reign. He divided the kingdom into twelve administrative districts, each overseen by an appointed governor responsible for collecting taxes and provisioning the royal court. This system helped to streamline governance and ensure a steady flow of resources to the central administration. Solomon's court, with its elaborate hierarchy and bureaucracy, reflected the complexity and sophistication of his administration. The descriptions of his officials, servants, and the daily provisions for the royal household in 1 Kings 4 provide a glimpse into the opulence and efficiency of his rule.

Despite these achievements, Solomon's reign was not without controversy and challenges. His extensive building projects and luxurious lifestyle placed a heavy burden on the populace. The labor and taxes required to support his endeavors led to growing discontent among the Israelites, particularly in the northern tribes. Additionally, Solomon's numerous marriages to foreign women, as part of diplomatic alliances, introduced the worship of foreign gods and idolatrous practices into Israel. According to the biblical narrative in 1 Kings 11, Solomon's wives turned his heart away from exclusive devotion to Yahweh, leading him to build high places for the gods of his wives. This apostasy, in turn, provoked divine displeasure and foreshadowed the eventual division of the kingdom.

The latter years of Solomon's reign were marked by internal strife and external threats. Rebellions arose, including the revolt of Jeroboam, who would later become the first king of the northern kingdom of Israel after Solomon's death. These internal divisions and the rising discontent set the stage for the fracturing of the united monarchy shortly after Solomon's death.

Solomon's death around 931 BCE marked the end of an era. His son Rehoboam succeeded him, but his harsh policies and inability to address the grievances of the northern tribes led to the secession of the ten northern tribes and the establishment of the independent kingdom of Israel, with Jeroboam as its king. This division resulted in the southern kingdom of Judah, ruled by Rehoboam, and the northern kingdom of Israel, a fragmentation that had profound and lasting implications for the history of the Israelites.

Solomon's legacy extends far beyond his historical reign. In Judaism, he is remembered as a wise and prosperous king whose reign represented the zenith of Israel's power and glory. His contributions to wisdom literature, particularly the Proverbs, Ecclesiastes, and the Song of Songs, continue to be revered and studied for their spiritual and philosophical insights. The Temple he built became the central focus of Jewish worship and identity until its destruction by the Babylonians in 586 BCE.

In Christianity, Solomon is often seen as a type of Christ, embodying wisdom and divine favor. Jesus referred to Solomon's wisdom and splendor in the Gospels, and the wisdom literature attributed to Solomon has been incorporated into Christian theology and moral teaching. Solomon's role as a builder of the Temple also prefigures the Christian understanding of Jesus as the cornerstone of the spiritual temple, the Church.

In Islam, Solomon (known as Sulayman) is venerated as a prophet and a king endowed with divine wisdom and authority. The Qur'an contains numerous stories about Solomon, highlighting his ability to communicate with animals and jinn, his role as a just ruler, and his devotion to God. Islamic tradition also emphasizes Solomon's wisdom and his construction of the Jerusalem Temple, which is linked to the broader Islamic reverence for Jerusalem as a holy city.

Solomon's story has also permeated various cultural and literary traditions. His legendary wisdom, wealth, and the grandeur of his court have inspired countless works of art, literature, and folklore. From medieval manuscripts and Renaissance paintings to modern novels and films, Solomon's life and reign continue to captivate the imagination of people around the world.

Chapter 7: Alexander the Great

Alexander the Great, born in 356 BCE in Pella, the ancient capital of Macedonia, remains one of history's most illustrious and influential figures. His life, spanning only 32 years, was marked by an unprecedented series of military conquests that created one of the largest empires in the ancient world. As the son of King Philip II and Queen Olympias, Alexander inherited not only the throne of Macedonia but also the ambition and skills that would drive him to achieve legendary status.

From a young age, Alexander was groomed for greatness. His education was supervised by Aristotle, one of the greatest philosophers of the time, who instilled in him a deep appreciation for Greek culture, philosophy, and sciences. Aristotle's teachings had a profound impact on Alexander, shaping his intellectual development and strategic thinking. Under Aristotle's guidance, Alexander developed a love for literature, particularly the works of Homer, whose epic poems "The Iliad" and "The Odyssey" would inspire him throughout his life. The legendary hero Achilles, in particular, became Alexander's role model.

Alexander's early exposure to military tactics and leadership also came from his father, King Philip II, who had transformed Macedonia into a formidable military power. Philip's innovations, including the development of the phalanx formation and the integration of cavalry and infantry tactics, provided Alexander with a robust military foundation. At the age of 16, Alexander demonstrated his military acumen by successfully suppressing a rebellion in the Maedi city of Thrace, which he renamed Alexandropolis.

Upon Philip II's assassination in 336 BCE, Alexander ascended to the throne at the age of 20. His immediate task was to consolidate his power and secure his kingdom. Facing internal dissent and external threats, Alexander acted swiftly and decisively. He eliminated potential rivals and secured the loyalty of the Macedonian nobility. He then turned his attention to the Greek city-states, which had been dominated by Macedonia since Philip's victory at the Battle of Chaeronea in 338 BCE. When Thebes and Athens revolted upon Philip's death, Alexander responded with a swift campaign that culminated in the destruction of Thebes, sending a clear message to other Greek states and securing his authority over Greece.

With Greece pacified, Alexander embarked on his most ambitious endeavor: the conquest of the Persian Empire. In 334 BCE, he crossed the Hellespont (modern-day Dardanelles) into Asia Minor with a well-prepared army of approximately 35,000 soldiers. His first major battle against the Persians took place at the Granicus River, where he secured a decisive victory that opened the way into Asia Minor. Alexander's strategy combined bold, direct assaults with cunning tactics, and his leadership on the battlefield inspired unwavering loyalty among his troops.

In 333 BCE, Alexander faced the Persian king Darius III at the Battle of Issus. Despite being heavily outnumbered, Alexander's tactical brilliance led to a resounding victory. Darius fled the battlefield, leaving behind his family, who were captured by Alexander but treated with great respect. This battle showcased Alexander's strategic ingenuity and his ability to exploit the weaknesses of his opponents. Following the victory at Issus, Alexander marched southward, systematically conquering the coastal cities of Phoenicia, including Tyre, and securing vital supply lines.

One of Alexander's most famous sieges was that of Tyre, which lasted for seven months in 332 BCE. Tyre was a heavily fortified island city, and its capture required innovative engineering and relentless determination. Alexander's forces built a causeway to breach the island's defenses, demonstrating his ability to overcome formidable obstacles. The fall of Tyre was a significant achievement, as it not only secured the eastern Mediterranean coast but also demonstrated Alexander's resolve and resourcefulness.

After securing the eastern Mediterranean, Alexander continued his campaign into Egypt, where he was welcomed as a liberator from Persian rule. In 331 BCE, he founded the city of Alexandria, which would become a major center of Hellenistic culture and learning. His time in Egypt also included a visit to the Oracle of Amun at Siwa Oasis, where he was declared the son of Zeus-Ammon, reinforcing his divine status and further legitimizing his rule.

The decisive encounter between Alexander and Darius III occurred at the Battle of Gaugamela in 331 BCE. Despite facing a numerically superior Persian army, Alexander's superior tactics and the disciplined Macedonian phalanx secured a decisive victory. Darius once again fled the battlefield, and Alexander pursued him, eventually leading to Darius's assassination by his own men. With Darius's death, Alexander effectively became the ruler of the Persian Empire, extending his dominion from Greece to Egypt and from the Mediterranean to the fringes of India.

Alexander's conquests continued eastward into the heart of the Persian Empire. He captured the key cities of Babylon, Susa, and Persepolis, where he famously burned the royal palace in a symbolic act of retribution for the Persian invasion of Greece a century earlier. His campaigns then led him into the rugged terrain of Central Asia, where he faced fierce resistance and embarked on a series of arduous campaigns to subdue the region. Alexander's determination to integrate his newly conquered territories was evident in his policy of founding cities, many of which were named Alexandria, to serve as administrative centers and spread Hellenistic culture.

In 327 BCE, Alexander launched his campaign into the Indian subcontinent, where he encountered the formidable kingdom of the Punjab. The Battle of the Hydaspes River in 326 BCE against King Porus was one of Alexander's most challenging battles. Despite the difficulties posed by the monsoon rains and the presence of war elephants, Alexander's tactical genius secured a hard-fought victory.

Impressed by Porus's valor, Alexander reinstated him as a regional ruler under his own suzerainty, demonstrating his capacity for both military might and diplomatic acumen.

Alexander's campaign in India, however, was marked by increasing resistance from his own troops, who were weary from years of continuous warfare and longed to return home. In 326 BCE, after reaching the Hyphasis River (modern Beas River), his army, exhausted and facing the prospect of further campaigns against the powerful Nanda Empire, mutinied. Reluctantly, Alexander agreed to turn back, leading his forces down the Indus River and through the harsh Gedrosian Desert, where they faced severe hardships.

Upon his return to Babylon in 324 BCE, Alexander began to consolidate his empire and implement policies aimed at integrating his diverse subjects. He encouraged marriages between his Macedonian soldiers and Persian women, symbolized by his own marriage to Roxana, a Bactrian princess. He also adopted elements of Persian dress and customs, which alienated some of his Macedonian followers but helped to bridge cultural divides within his empire.

Alexander's final months were consumed by plans for further military campaigns, including an ambitious expedition to Arabia. However, these plans were cut short when he fell ill in Babylon in 323 BCE. His sudden death, possibly due to fever, poisoning, or other causes, left a power vacuum and plunged his empire into chaos. Without a clear successor, his generals, known as the Diadochi, engaged in a series of wars to carve out their own kingdoms from Alexander's vast territories, leading to the fragmentation of his empire.

Despite the disintegration of his empire, Alexander's legacy endured in numerous ways. The Hellenistic period that followed his death saw the spread of Greek culture, language, and ideas throughout the Mediterranean, Near East, and parts of Asia. The cities he founded became centers of learning and cultural exchange, blending Greek and local traditions. Alexandria in Egypt, in particular, became a renowned center of scholarship, home to the famous Library of Alexandria.

Alexander's conquests also facilitated the exchange of goods, ideas, and technologies between East and West. His campaigns opened up new trade routes and fostered connections between diverse civilizations. The diffusion of Greek culture, combined with local traditions, led to significant developments in art, science, philosophy, and architecture. The Hellenistic influence can be seen in the blending of artistic styles, the spread of Greek language and literature, and the establishment of Greco-Buddhist art in regions as far as Gandhara (modern-day Pakistan and Afghanistan).

In the realm of military strategy, Alexander's tactics and innovations had a lasting impact on warfare. His use of the phalanx formation, combined with cavalry maneuvers and siege techniques, set new standards for military campaigns. Future military leaders, from Julius Caesar to Napoleon Bonaparte, studied and emulated his strategies, recognizing his unparalleled skill as a commander.

Alexander's persona and achievements also left an indelible mark on the cultural imagination. He was celebrated in numerous works of literature, from the Greek "Alexander Romance" to Persian and Arabic legends, where he is often referred to as Iskandar. These stories, sometimes embellished and mythologized, contributed to his enduring legacy as a larger-than-life figure who transcended cultural boundaries.

Chapter 8: Ashoka the Great

Ashoka the Great, also known as Ashoka Maurya, was an Indian emperor of the Maurya Dynasty who reigned from approximately 268 to 232 BCE. His reign is often considered one of the most illustrious periods in Indian history, marked by profound transformation and monumental achievements. Ashoka's legacy is multifaceted, encompassing his military conquests, his embrace and promotion of Buddhism, his administrative innovations, and his efforts to create a just and moral society. His life and reign have left an indelible impact on the Indian subcontinent and beyond, earning him a place as one of history's most enlightened rulers.

Born around 304 BCE, Ashoka was the grandson of Chandragupta Maurya, the founder of the Maurya Dynasty, and the son of Bindusara. From an early age, Ashoka exhibited signs of exceptional intelligence and capability, which earned him the attention and favor of his father. However, his path to the throne was neither straightforward nor peaceful. The Mauryan court was rife with intrigue and rivalry, and Ashoka had to navigate a complex and often dangerous political landscape. According to some historical accounts, Ashoka's ascension to power involved a series of violent purges, during which he eliminated potential rivals, including his brothers. These actions earned him the nickname "Ashoka the Fierce."

Upon securing his position as emperor, Ashoka initially continued the expansionist policies of his predecessors. One of the most significant events in Ashoka's early reign was the conquest of the Kalinga region (modern-day Odisha) around 260 BCE. The Kalinga War, as it came to be known, was a brutal and bloody conflict. According to Ashoka's own inscriptions, the war resulted in the death of over 100,000 soldiers and civilians, and more than 150,000 people were displaced. The sheer scale of the devastation and human suffering left a profound impact on Ashoka, leading to a pivotal transformation in his outlook and policies.

Deeply moved by the horrors of the Kalinga War, Ashoka underwent a personal and moral awakening. He publicly expressed his remorse and sorrow for the suffering caused by the conflict. This moment of epiphany marked a dramatic shift in his reign and the beginning of his embrace of Buddhism. Ashoka's conversion to Buddhism was not merely a personal spiritual journey but also a significant turning point in Indian history. He became a fervent patron of Buddhism, dedicating himself to the propagation of its teachings and principles throughout his empire and beyond.

Ashoka's commitment to Buddhism was reflected in his policies and governance. He renounced further military conquests and adopted a policy of Dhamma (Dharma), which emphasized non-violence, tolerance, compassion, and moral living. Ashoka's Dhamma was a synthesis of Buddhist teachings and ethical principles aimed at creating a just and harmonious society. He believed that the well-being of his subjects and the moral fabric of the empire were paramount, and he implemented a range of reforms to promote these values.

One of Ashoka's most enduring legacies is his extensive use of inscriptions and edicts to communicate his policies and moral principles. These inscriptions, known as the Edicts of Ashoka, were carved on rocks, pillars, and cave walls across the Indian subcontinent. Written in various languages, including Prakrit, Greek, and Aramaic, the edicts served as public proclamations of Ashoka's vision of governance and his commitment to Dhamma. They addressed a wide range of topics, including the promotion of non-violence, the welfare of his subjects, religious tolerance, and the fair treatment of prisoners and animals.

The Rock and Pillar Edicts of Ashoka are among the most significant historical sources for understanding his reign and philosophy. The edicts reveal a ruler deeply concerned with the moral and spiritual welfare of his people. For instance, in Rock Edict XIII, Ashoka expresses his profound regret for the suffering caused by the Kalinga War and his commitment to the propagation of Dhamma as a means of ensuring peace and harmony. Pillar Edict VII emphasizes Ashoka's dedication to the welfare of all beings, including humans and animals, and his efforts to provide medical care and establish rest houses for travelers.

Ashoka's promotion of Buddhism extended beyond the borders of his empire. He sent missionaries to various parts of Asia, including Sri Lanka, Central Asia, and the Hellenistic kingdoms in the West. These missions played a crucial role in the spread of Buddhism, helping to establish it as a major world religion. Ashoka's son, Mahinda, and daughter, Sanghamitta, are traditionally credited with introducing Buddhism to Sri Lanka, where it took root and flourished. The impact of Ashoka's missionary efforts is evident in the widespread adoption of Buddhism across Asia and its enduring influence on the cultures and societies of the region.

In addition to his religious and moral reforms, Ashoka implemented significant administrative and infrastructural changes aimed at improving the lives of his subjects. He established a network of roads and built rest houses, wells, and hospitals throughout the empire to facilitate travel, trade, and the provision of medical care. These public works projects not only enhanced the economic and social well-being of the population but also demonstrated Ashoka's commitment to the welfare of his people.

Ashoka's administration was marked by a spirit of inclusiveness and religious tolerance. He encouraged respect and coexistence among different religious communities, including Buddhists, Hindus, Jains, and others. This policy of religious tolerance is evident in several of his edicts, where he emphasizes the importance of understanding and respecting other faiths. Ashoka's approach to governance reflected his belief that moral and ethical principles should guide political and social life, transcending sectarian divisions.

Despite his emphasis on non-violence and moral governance, Ashoka maintained a well-organized and efficient administration. He appointed officials known as Dhamma Mahamatras to oversee the implementation of his policies and ensure that his edicts were followed. These officials were responsible for promoting Dhamma, resolving disputes, and protecting the rights of the vulnerable, including prisoners, slaves, and animals. Ashoka's administrative reforms helped to create a stable and well-governed empire that endured for several generations after his death.

Ashoka's reign also had a significant impact on the cultural and artistic landscape of the Mauryan Empire. He commissioned the construction of numerous stupas, monasteries, and other Buddhist monuments, many of which became important centers of pilgrimage and learning. The Great Stupa at Sanchi, one of the most famous and well-preserved examples of Mauryan architecture, was originally commissioned by Ashoka and later expanded by subsequent rulers. These architectural achievements not only served as expressions of Ashoka's devotion to Buddhism but also contributed to the cultural and artistic heritage of India.

The legacy of Ashoka the Great extends far beyond his reign. His vision of a just and moral society, his promotion of religious tolerance, and his efforts to improve the welfare of his people have left an enduring mark on Indian history and culture. Ashoka's embrace of Buddhism and his efforts to spread its teachings helped to shape the religious and philosophical landscape of Asia. His edicts, inscribed on rocks and pillars across the subcontinent, remain a testament to his commitment to Dhamma and his vision of ethical governance.

In the centuries following Ashoka's death, his legacy continued to inspire rulers and thinkers across Asia. The concept of Dhamma, as articulated by Ashoka, influenced subsequent Indian dynasties, including the Gupta Empire, which saw a resurgence of Buddhism and a renewed emphasis on ethical governance. Ashoka's legacy also reached beyond India, influencing the development of Buddhist thought and practice in regions such as Sri Lanka, Southeast Asia, and Central Asia.

Ashoka's story was largely forgotten in India for many centuries, but it was rediscovered in the 19th century through the efforts of British archaeologists and scholars. The decipherment of the Brahmi script, used in Ashoka's edicts, by James Prinsep in the 1830s revealed the richness of Ashoka's contributions to Indian history. Today, Ashoka is celebrated as one of India's greatest rulers, and his legacy is commemorated in various ways, including the adoption of the Ashoka Chakra (the wheel of law) as a central symbol in the national flag of India.

Chapter 9: Qin Shi Huang

Qin Shi Huang, born Ying Zheng in 259 BCE, was the first emperor of a unified China and the founder of the Qin Dynasty. His reign, which lasted from 221 BCE until his death in 210 BCE, was a transformative period in Chinese history, marked by monumental achievements and profound changes in political, cultural, and social structures. Qin Shi Huang's legacy is both celebrated for his unification of China and criticized for his autocratic rule and harsh measures. His ambitious projects, including the construction of the Great Wall and his elaborate mausoleum guarded by the Terracotta Army, continue to captivate the imagination of historians and the general public alike.

Ying Zheng was born to King Zhuangxiang of Qin and a concubine named Zhao Ji. His early life was shaped by the political turmoil and intrigue of the Warring States period, a time when seven major states—Qin, Qi, Chu, Yan, Han, Zhao, and Wei—were vying for dominance over China. At the age of 13, Ying Zheng ascended to the throne of Qin following his father's death. Due to his youth, the state was initially governed by regents, including the influential Chancellor Lü Buwei, who is rumored by some sources to have been Ying Zheng's biological father. When Ying Zheng reached adulthood, he assumed full control of the state and embarked on a series of military campaigns and political reforms aimed at consolidating his power and unifying China.

The state of Qin, located in the western part of China, had long been considered a formidable military power. Under Ying Zheng's leadership, Qin's military prowess was further enhanced by innovative strategies and the use of iron weapons and crossbows. From 230 BCE to 221 BCE, Ying Zheng launched a series of aggressive campaigns against the other warring states. His generals, including the renowned Wang Jian and Meng Tian, played crucial roles in these conquests. The fall of the Han state in 230 BCE marked the beginning of Qin's dominance, followed by Zhao in 228 BCE, Wei in 225 BCE, Chu in 223 BCE, Yan in 222 BCE, and finally Qi in 221 BCE. With these victories, Ying Zheng succeeded in unifying China for the first time in its history, declaring himself Qin Shi Huang, which means "First Emperor of Qin."

Qin Shi Huang's unification of China was a monumental achievement, but it was only the beginning of his transformative reign. Recognizing the need to consolidate his rule over a vast and diverse territory, he implemented a series of sweeping reforms that fundamentally altered the political, economic, and social landscape of China. One of his most significant reforms was the centralization of power. He abolished the feudal system that had characterized the Warring States period, replacing it with a centralized bureaucratic system. The empire was divided into 36 commanderies (jun), each governed by officials appointed by the emperor. This system helped to reduce the power of local nobility and ensured that loyalty was directed towards the central government.

To further strengthen central authority, Qin Shi Huang standardized various aspects of Chinese society. He introduced a uniform legal code based on the principles of Legalism, a philosophy that emphasized strict laws and harsh punishments to maintain order and control. Legalist scholars like Han Feizi influenced the emperor's policies, which were characterized by their severity. While these measures helped to maintain stability and deter rebellion, they also contributed to the perception of Qin Shi Huang as a ruthless and tyrannical ruler.

Standardization extended beyond the legal system. Qin Shi Huang introduced standardized weights and measures, currency, and even the writing system. The standardization of the written script was particularly significant, as it facilitated communication and administration across the vast empire. The small seal script, developed under the emperor's orders, became the official script for government and legal documents, reducing regional linguistic variations and promoting unity.

Qin Shi Huang also embarked on massive infrastructure projects that showcased his ambition and vision. One of the most famous of these projects was the construction of the Great Wall of China. Originally built to protect the northern borders from nomadic invasions, the Great Wall was an enormous undertaking that required the labor of hundreds of thousands of workers, many of whom were conscripted peasants and prisoners. The wall, constructed using a combination of tamped earth and later stone and bricks, stretched over 5,000 kilometers. While the Great Wall was not completed in its entirety during Qin Shi Huang's reign, his efforts laid the foundation for future expansions and fortifications.

Another significant project was the construction of an extensive network of roads and canals to improve transportation and communication across the empire. The most notable of these was the Straight Road, which connected the capital Xianyang with the northern frontier. This road facilitated the movement of troops, goods, and information, enhancing the emperor's control over distant regions. The Lingqu Canal, built to connect the Xiang and Li rivers, exemplified Qin Shi Huang's engineering prowess and contributed to the integration of southern China into the empire.

Qin Shi Huang's capital city, Xianyang, was transformed into a magnificent center of power. The city was adorned with grand palaces, administrative buildings, and other structures designed to reflect the emperor's authority and the grandeur of his rule. The architectural achievements of the Qin Dynasty, although many have not survived the passage of time, were remarkable and set the stage for future developments in Chinese architecture and urban planning.

One of the most enduring and fascinating aspects of Qin Shi Huang's legacy is his mausoleum, which is located near modern-day Xi'an in Shaanxi province. The mausoleum, a massive complex covering approximately 56 square kilometers, was designed to mirror the layout of the capital city and to provide the emperor with a grand resting place in the afterlife. The most famous feature of the mausoleum is the Terracotta Army, an astonishing collection of thousands of life-sized clay soldiers, horses, and chariots buried with the emperor. Discovered in 1974 by local farmers, the Terracotta Army was intended to protect Qin Shi Huang in the afterlife and reflects the emperor's belief in his eternal rule. The level of detail and craftsmanship in the figures, each with unique facial features and expressions, is a testament to the skill of the artisans and the resources devoted to the project.

Despite his many achievements, Qin Shi Huang's reign was also marked by severe repression and widespread discontent. His autocratic rule, characterized by strict enforcement of laws and harsh punishments, led to significant suffering among the populace. The construction of grandiose projects like the Great Wall and the emperor's mausoleum required immense human labor, often obtained through forced conscription. The heavy taxation and conscription policies caused widespread resentment, and the emperor's efforts to suppress dissent were brutal. In one infamous episode, known as the burning of books and burying of scholars, Qin Shi Huang ordered the destruction of numerous texts and the execution of Confucian scholars who opposed his policies. This act of cultural repression was intended to eliminate ideological opposition and consolidate the emperor's control over knowledge and education.

Qin Shi Huang's obsession with immortality also played a significant role in his later years. Driven by a fear of death and a desire to achieve eternal life, he embarked on numerous quests to find elixirs of immortality. The emperor sent expeditions to distant lands in search of mythical substances and consulted alchemists and magicians who promised to extend his life. These efforts, however, were ultimately futile and may have contributed to his declining health.

In 210 BCE, while on a tour of his empire, Qin Shi Huang fell seriously ill and died. His death was followed by a power struggle among his officials and family members. The emperor's death marked the beginning of the end for the Qin Dynasty. The harsh policies and heavy burdens imposed by Qin Shi Huang had left the empire vulnerable to unrest. His son, Qin Er Shi, succeeded him but was unable to maintain control. Within a few years, widespread rebellions erupted, leading to the fall of the Qin Dynasty in 206 BCE. The Han Dynasty, which followed, adopted many of the administrative innovations introduced by Qin Shi Huang but also sought to distance itself from the more oppressive aspects of his rule.

Qin Shi Huang's legacy is complex and multifaceted. On one hand, he is remembered as a visionary leader who achieved the monumental feat of unifying China and laying the foundations for a centralized state. His reforms in administration, standardization, and infrastructure had a lasting impact on Chinese civilization. On the other hand, his autocratic rule, characterized by severe repression and harsh measures, has led to a more critical assessment of his reign. The suffering endured by the people during his ambitious projects and the cultural repression he imposed cast a shadow over his accomplishments.

In modern times, Qin Shi Huang's legacy continues to be a subject of fascination and debate. His life and achievements have been the inspiration for numerous books, films, and academic studies. The discovery of the Terracotta Army has brought renewed attention to his reign and has provided valuable insights into the art, culture, and military practices of ancient China. The site of his mausoleum has become a major archaeological and tourist attraction, drawing millions of visitors from around the world.

Chapter 10: Julius Caesar

Gaius Julius Caesar, born in 100 BCE and assassinated in 44 BCE, was a towering figure in Roman history. His life, marked by military conquests, political maneuvers, and a profound transformation of the Roman Republic, has been extensively documented and analyzed, making him one of the most iconic figures of classical antiquity. Caesar's rise to power, his role in the end of the Roman Republic, and his assassination have left an indelible mark on history, shaping the course of Western civilization.

Caesar was born into the patrician Julian family, which claimed descent from Iulus, the son of the Trojan prince Aeneas, who was purportedly the son of the goddess Venus. Despite this illustrious lineage, the Julii Caesares were not particularly influential during Caesar's early years. However, the political turmoil and civil wars of the late Republic provided opportunities for ambitious individuals like Caesar to rise to prominence.

From a young age, Caesar displayed exceptional talent and ambition. His political career began in the tumultuous environment of the late Republic, where he aligned himself with the popularis faction, which advocated for the rights of the common people against the optimates, the conservative senatorial aristocracy. This alignment with the populares was a strategic move that helped Caesar gain the support of the masses, crucial for his future endeavors.

In 84 BCE, at the age of 16, Caesar's life took a significant turn when he married Cornelia, the daughter of Lucius Cornelius Cinna, a leading figure of the popularis faction and an opponent of the dictator Sulla. This marriage placed Caesar in direct opposition to Sulla, who had seized control of Rome and was systematically purging his enemies. Sulla ordered Caesar to divorce Cornelia, but Caesar refused, displaying his characteristic resolve and defiance. Although Sulla eventually relented and spared his life, Caesar was forced to go into hiding and serve in the military to avoid further persecution.

Caesar's military service in Asia Minor and Cilicia was the first step in his illustrious career. His bravery and leadership skills were evident in his early military engagements, earning him the prestigious Civic Crown for saving the life of a fellow soldier. These early experiences not only honed his military abilities but also helped him build crucial alliances and a network of supporters.

After Sulla's death in 78 BCE, Caesar returned to Rome and embarked on a political career. He held various minor offices before being elected as a quaestor in 69 BCE, which marked his entry into the Roman Senate. Around this time, he delivered the funeral oration for his aunt Julia, the widow of the famous general Marius, further solidifying his connections to the popularis cause. In 65 BCE, Caesar was elected as curule aedile, a position that allowed him to gain public favor through lavish games and public spectacles.

Caesar's political ascent continued with his election as pontifex maximus, the chief priest of the Roman state religion, in 63 BCE. This position not only increased his prestige but also provided him with significant religious and political influence. The following year, he was elected as praetor, one of the senior magistrates of the Republic. These successive offices demonstrated his growing power and influence within the Roman political system.

In 61 BCE, Caesar was appointed governor of Hispania Ulterior (Further Spain), where his military and administrative talents came to the fore. He subdued rebellious tribes and secured substantial spoils, which alleviated his considerable debts. His success in Spain set the stage for his return to Rome, where he sought to further his political career.

Upon his return to Rome in 60 BCE, Caesar formed the First Triumvirate with Pompey and Crassus, two of the most powerful men in Rome. This informal political alliance was based on mutual benefit:

Pompey sought land for his veterans, Crassus needed political support for his financial ventures, and Caesar required backing to secure his consulship and subsequent provincial command. The Triumvirate effectively dominated Roman politics, bypassing the traditional senatorial opposition.

As consul in 59 BCE, Caesar enacted a series of reforms that benefited his allies and himself. He pushed through land reforms for Pompey's veterans and secured lucrative provincial governorships for his future campaigns. His tenure as consul was marked by his ability to navigate the complex political landscape, often using unorthodox methods to achieve his goals.

After his consulship, Caesar was appointed governor of Cisalpine Gaul, Transalpine Gaul, and Illyricum for an unprecedented five-year term. This command provided him with the resources and autonomy to embark on one of the most significant military campaigns in Roman history: the Gallic Wars. From 58 to 50 BCE, Caesar waged a series of campaigns against various Gallic tribes, expanding Roman territory to the Atlantic Ocean.

The Gallic Wars showcased Caesar's military genius and established him as one of Rome's greatest generals. He demonstrated exceptional strategic and tactical skills, often achieving victory against numerically superior forces. Notable battles included the defeat of the Helvetii, the conquest of the Belgic tribes, and the famous siege of Alesia, where he captured the Gallic leader Vercingetorix. The campaigns not only enriched Caesar and his soldiers but also secured his reputation and increased his political power.

However, Caesar's growing power and popularity alarmed many in the Senate, particularly his former ally Pompey, who had shifted allegiances to the optimates. The rivalry between Caesar and Pompey escalated, culminating in the Senate's demand for Caesar to disband his army and return to Rome as a private citizen. Caesar's refusal to comply led to a declaration of war.

In 49 BCE, Caesar crossed the Rubicon River with his army, uttering the famous phrase "Alea iacta est" ("The die is cast"). This act of defiance against the Senate marked the beginning of the Roman Civil War. Over the next few years, Caesar's forces engaged in a series of battles against Pompey's legions, with the decisive confrontation occurring at the Battle of Pharsalus in 48 BCE. Despite being outnumbered, Caesar's tactical brilliance secured a decisive victory, forcing Pompey to flee to Egypt, where he was eventually assassinated.

Following his victory in the civil war, Caesar pursued Pompey's supporters to various parts of the Mediterranean, securing his dominance over the Roman world. His campaigns took him to Egypt, where he became involved in the country's dynastic struggles, supporting Cleopatra VII in her bid for the throne. Caesar's liaison with Cleopatra resulted in a son, Ptolemy XV, known as Caesarion. His time in Egypt further demonstrated his political acumen and his ability to adapt to diverse cultural contexts.

Returning to Rome in 46 BCE, Caesar was appointed dictator, a position he held for an unprecedented period. He embarked on a comprehensive program of reforms aimed at stabilizing and revitalizing the Roman state. These reforms included the reorganization of the calendar, resulting in the Julian calendar, which closely resembles the modern Gregorian calendar. He also initiated social and economic reforms, such as debt relief, land redistribution, and the establishment of colonies for veterans.

Despite his reforms, Caesar's accumulation of power and his title of "dictator perpetuo" (dictator in perpetuity) generated significant opposition among certain factions of the Senate. Many senators feared that Caesar aimed to establish a monarchy, undermining the republican traditions of Rome. This opposition culminated in a conspiracy led by senators Brutus and Cassius, who believed that Caesar's death was necessary to restore the Republic.

On the Ides of March, March 15, 44 BCE, Caesar was assassinated in the Senate House. He was stabbed 23 times by a group of conspirators, including many whom he considered friends. His assassination plunged Rome into further turmoil and set the stage for the end of the Roman Republic. The ensuing power struggle among Caesar's supporters and opponents led to the rise of the Second Triumvirate—comprising Octavian (later Augustus), Mark Antony, and Lepidus—and eventually the establishment of the Roman Empire under Augustus.

Caesar's legacy is profound and multifaceted. He is remembered as one of history's greatest military commanders, whose conquests expanded the boundaries of the Roman state and brought immense wealth and prestige. His political reforms and centralization of power laid the groundwork for the transition from Republic to Empire, although his concentration of authority also highlighted the inherent weaknesses and contradictions within the republican system.

His writings, particularly "Commentarii de Bello Gallico" (Commentaries on the Gallic War), provide invaluable insights into his military campaigns and serve as classic examples of Latin prose. These commentaries not only chronicle his achievements but also reflect his skill as a propagandist, shaping his public image and legacy.

In modern times, Julius Caesar's life and legacy continue to be the subject of extensive study and popular interest. His impact on Roman history and Western civilization is undeniable, influencing political thought, literature, and culture. The Shakespearean play "Julius Caesar," for instance, immortalizes his assassination and the political intrigue of his time, contributing to the enduring fascination with his character and era.

Chapter 11: Cleopatra VII of Egypt

Cleopatra VII Thea Philopator, commonly known as Cleopatra, was the last active ruler of the Ptolemaic Kingdom of Egypt. Born in 69 BCE and dying in 30 BCE, her life and reign were marked by political intrigue, romantic liaisons, and dramatic events that have captivated historians and inspired countless works of art, literature, and film. Cleopatra's efforts to preserve her kingdom's independence amidst the expanding power of Rome, her relationships with key Roman figures like Julius Caesar and Mark Antony, and her ultimate tragic demise have made her one of the most iconic figures of antiquity.

Cleopatra was born into the Ptolemaic dynasty, a Macedonian Greek royal family that ruled Egypt following the death of Alexander the Great. Her father, Ptolemy XII Auletes, was the reigning pharaoh. Despite the dynasty's Greek origins, Cleopatra was notably the first of her line to learn the Egyptian language, and she adopted many Egyptian customs, portraying herself as the reincarnation of the goddess Isis. This ability to blend cultures and appeal to both Greek and Egyptian subjects would be a hallmark of her reign.

When Ptolemy XII died in 51 BCE, the throne passed to Cleopatra and her younger brother Ptolemy XIII, whom she married according to Egyptian custom. Initially, Cleopatra was the dominant ruler, but tensions quickly arose between her and Ptolemy XIII. In 48 BCE, these tensions erupted into civil war, leading Cleopatra to flee to Syria to gather an army. During this time, Julius Caesar, the Roman general and statesman, arrived in Egypt pursuing his rival Pompey the Great.

Cleopatra seized this opportunity to align herself with Caesar, famously having herself smuggled into the palace rolled up in a carpet to meet him. Captivated by her intelligence, charm, and political acumen, Caesar became her ally and lover. He helped her defeat Ptolemy XIII, who drowned in the Nile during the conflict. Cleopatra was then restored to the throne, this time ruling alongside her younger brother Ptolemy XIV, whom she also married.

In 47 BCE, Cleopatra gave birth to a son, Ptolemy XV, nicknamed Caesarion, meaning "little Caesar." Although Caesar never publicly acknowledged him as his son, it was widely believed that he was the father. Cleopatra's relationship with Caesar strengthened her position, but it also tied her fate closely to his.

Following Caesar's assassination in 44 BCE, Cleopatra returned to Egypt. The political situation in Rome was chaotic, with power struggles leading to the formation of the Second Triumvirate, composed of Octavian (later Augustus), Mark Antony, and Lepidus. Cleopatra aligned herself with Mark Antony, who controlled Rome's eastern territories. Their relationship was both political and romantic, and they had three children together: twins Alexander Helios and Cleopatra Selene, and a son named Ptolemy Philadelphus.

Mark Antony and Cleopatra's alliance was a direct challenge to Octavian's power, leading to a propaganda war. Octavian portrayed Cleopatra as a seductive foreign queen who had bewitched Antony, undermining his Roman values and ambitions. The tension culminated in the naval Battle of Actium in 31 BCE. Cleopatra and Antony's forces were decisively defeated by Octavian's fleet, commanded by Agrippa. Following the defeat, Antony and Cleopatra retreated to Alexandria.

In August 30 BCE, as Octavian's forces closed in on Alexandria, both Antony and Cleopatra chose to commit suicide rather than be captured. Antony died by his own sword, while Cleopatra is said to have allowed herself to be bitten by an asp, though the exact method of her death remains a topic of speculation. With their deaths, Egypt fell to Rome, and Caesarion was captured and executed. Cleopatra's other children were taken to Rome and raised by Octavian's sister, Octavia Minor.

Cleopatra's reign marked the end of the Hellenistic period and the beginning of Roman domination in the eastern Mediterranean. Despite the fall of her kingdom, her legacy endured. Cleopatra was a shrewd and competent ruler who sought to maintain Egypt's independence through strategic alliances and bold political maneuvers. Her ability to navigate the complex political landscape of her time was remarkable, as was her skill in using her charm and intellect to forge powerful alliances.

Cleopatra's life has been romanticized and mythologized over the centuries. Ancient sources, including the Roman historians Plutarch and Dio Cassius, often portrayed her as a femme fatale whose beauty and seduction led to the downfall of powerful men. However, modern scholarship has sought to present a more balanced view, emphasizing her political acumen, linguistic skills, and effective governance.

Cleopatra was highly educated, having studied with the best tutors of her time. She spoke several languages, including Greek, Egyptian, and likely others such as Aramaic and Latin. This linguistic proficiency allowed her to communicate directly with various ethnic groups within her kingdom and with foreign dignitaries. Her education and intelligence were key to her ability to rule a diverse and complex society.

In addition to her political and linguistic skills, Cleopatra was a patron of the arts and sciences. Alexandria, the capital of her kingdom, was a major center of learning and culture, home to the famous Library of Alexandria. Cleopatra supported scholars, poets, and scientists, fostering an environment of intellectual exchange and creativity.

Cleopatra's efforts to stabilize and strengthen her kingdom included economic and administrative reforms. She took measures to improve agriculture, enhance trade, and manage the economy more effectively. Her policies aimed to ensure the prosperity of Egypt and secure its position as a vital economic hub in the Mediterranean world.

Despite her efforts, Cleopatra's reign was fraught with challenges. The internal political strife within her own family, the constant threat of Roman intervention, and the broader geopolitical dynamics of the time created a volatile environment. Her alliances with Julius Caesar and Mark Antony were strategic moves to safeguard her kingdom's autonomy, but they also tied her fate to the shifting fortunes of Roman politics.

Cleopatra's dramatic life and death have inspired numerous works of art, literature, and film. She has been depicted in various ways, from the enchanting seductress to the wise and capable monarch. One of the most famous portrayals is William Shakespeare's play "Antony and Cleopatra," which explores the complexities of her relationships with Caesar and Antony and the tragic end of her reign.

In modern times, Cleopatra remains a subject of fascination and debate. Her legacy is often viewed through the lens of gender and power dynamics, as she was one of the few female rulers in a male-dominated world. Her story challenges traditional narratives of female power and influence, offering a compelling example of a woman who wielded significant political and cultural authority.

The fascination with Cleopatra extends beyond her historical role to her cultural and symbolic significance. She embodies themes of love, power, and betrayal, and her life story continues to resonate with contemporary audiences. The enduring interest in her life reflects broader questions about the nature of leadership, the interplay between personal and political ambitions, and the impact of historical narratives on our understanding of the past.

Chapter 12: Augustus Caesar

Augustus Caesar, born Gaius Octavius Thurinus on September 23, 63 BCE, was the founder of the Roman Empire and its first Emperor, ruling from 27 BCE until his death in 14 CE. His rise to power marked the end of the Roman Republic and the beginning of an era of imperial rule that would last for centuries. Augustus' reign was characterized by a combination of military prowess, political acumen, and extensive reforms that transformed Rome and laid the foundation for the Pax Romana, a period of relative peace and stability across the empire. His life and legacy remain central to the study of Roman history, highlighting the transition from republican to imperial governance.

Augustus was born into the gens Octavia, a plebeian family that had risen to prominence in Roman society. His father, also named Gaius Octavius, was a senator and governor, while his mother, Atia Balba Caesonia, was the niece of Julius Caesar. Despite his relatively modest beginnings, Augustus' connection to Caesar would prove pivotal in his ascent to power. After his father's death in 58 BCE, Augustus was raised by his mother and stepfather, Lucius Marcius Philippus. His education was typical for a young Roman of his status, including studies in rhetoric, philosophy, and the art of war.

In 44 BCE, when Julius Caesar was assassinated, Augustus was studying in Apollonia, Illyricum (modern-day Albania). Caesar's will named him as his adopted son and heir, a fact that catapulted the young Octavius into the center of Roman politics. Upon returning to Rome, he accepted his inheritance, taking the name Gaius Julius Caesar Octavianus (Octavian). At just 18 years old, Octavian faced a turbulent political landscape dominated by Caesar's assassins and his rival Mark Antony.

The power vacuum left by Caesar's death led to the formation of the Second Triumvirate in 43 BCE, an alliance between Octavian, Mark Antony, and Marcus Aemilius Lepidus. This triumvirate was officially sanctioned by the Lex Titia, which granted the three men extraordinary powers to restore order to the Republic. The triumvirs launched a campaign against Caesar's assassins, culminating in the Battle of Philippi in 42 BCE, where they decisively defeated the forces of Brutus and Cassius.

Following their victory, the triumvirs divided the Roman territories among themselves: Antony took the East, Lepidus the West, and Octavian the provinces of Africa and the Western Mediterranean. However, the alliance was fraught with tension, particularly between Octavian and Antony. Antony's romantic and political alliance with Cleopatra VII of Egypt exacerbated these tensions, leading to a propaganda war between Octavian and Antony. Octavian skillfully depicted Antony as a traitor to Rome who had succumbed to the wiles of a foreign queen.

The rivalry between Octavian and Antony culminated in the naval Battle of Actium in 31 BCE. Octavian's fleet, commanded by his trusted general Agrippa, defeated Antony and Cleopatra's forces, leading to their eventual suicides in Alexandria in 30 BCE. With their deaths, Octavian became the undisputed master of the Roman world.

In 27 BCE, Octavian offered to relinquish his extraordinary powers and restore the Republic, but the Senate, likely influenced by his supporters, instead granted him unprecedented authority. He was awarded the title Augustus, meaning "the revered one," and took the name Imperator Caesar Divi Filius Augustus. This event marked the beginning of the Roman Empire, with Augustus as its first Emperor. His new titles and powers included princeps senatus (first citizen of the Senate), imperator (commander-in-chief), and pontifex maximus (chief priest), consolidating his control over the military, religious, and political spheres.

Augustus' reign initiated a series of reforms that stabilized and strengthened the Roman state. His administrative changes included the creation of a professional standing army, the establishment of the

Praetorian Guard as his personal bodyguard, and the reorganization of the provinces. He implemented a census and reformed the tax system to ensure more efficient revenue collection. These measures not only secured his power but also brought a degree of order and predictability to the governance of the empire.

The Pax Romana, or Roman Peace, was one of Augustus' most significant achievements. This period, lasting roughly 200 years, was characterized by relative peace, economic prosperity, and cultural flourishing. Augustus' policies promoted trade, improved infrastructure, and encouraged the arts. His reign saw the construction of numerous public buildings, roads, and aqueducts, many of which stood for centuries as testaments to the architectural and engineering prowess of the Romans.

Augustus was also a patron of the arts and literature. His reign saw the flourishing of Roman literature, with poets like Virgil, Horace, and Ovid producing works that became classics of Western literature. The Aeneid, Virgil's epic poem, was written under Augustus' patronage and served to link Rome's origins with the divine and heroic past, further legitimizing Augustus' rule.

Religious and moral reforms were another key aspect of Augustus' reign. He sought to revive traditional Roman religious practices and values, which he believed had been eroded during the tumultuous final years of the Republic. Augustus restored temples, promoted the worship of the Roman gods, and emphasized the importance of family values and social morality. His legislation encouraged marriage and childbearing among the elite and penalized adultery and celibacy, aiming to strengthen the social fabric of Rome.

Despite his authoritarian rule, Augustus maintained the façade of republican governance. He was careful to present himself as the first among equals (princeps) rather than a monarch. The Senate continued to function, and traditional republican offices were maintained, although their real power was significantly diminished. This balance of autocratic control with republican traditions helped to legitimize his rule and prevent significant opposition.

Augustus' succession plans were carefully managed to ensure the stability of the empire. His chosen successor was initially his nephew Marcellus, but Marcellus' early death forced Augustus to reconsider. He then turned to his trusted friend Agrippa, who married Augustus' daughter Julia and fathered several children, including Gaius and Lucius Caesar. After Agrippa's death, Augustus adopted his stepson Tiberius, who ultimately succeeded him as Emperor.

In his later years, Augustus faced several challenges, including military revolts, a disastrous defeat in the Teutoburg Forest in 9 CE, and personal tragedies, such as the exile of his daughter Julia for adultery. Despite these difficulties, he maintained his grip on power and continued to implement reforms until his death.

Augustus died on August 19, 14 CE, at the age of 75. His death marked the end of an era, but the systems and structures he established ensured the continuity of the Roman Empire. The Senate declared him a god, and he was succeeded by Tiberius, who continued many of Augustus' policies.

The legacy of Augustus is profound and multifaceted. As the founder of the Roman Empire, his impact on Roman history is unparalleled. He transformed Rome from a fractious republic into a stable autocratic regime, initiating an era of peace and prosperity that would shape the ancient world for centuries. His administrative, military, and cultural reforms laid the foundations for the empire's longevity, and his legacy as a ruler who balanced power with pragmatism continues to be studied and admired.

Augustus' life and reign are a testament to his extraordinary political and military skills. He navigated the complex and often dangerous world of Roman politics with unmatched acumen, consolidating power while maintaining the appearance of republican governance. His ability to adapt and innovate ensured his success and the stability of his regime. His vision for Rome, articulated through his reforms and policies, created a legacy that would influence subsequent generations and shape the course of Western history.

The era of Augustus also highlights the transformation of Roman society and culture. Under his rule, Rome experienced a cultural renaissance, with advancements in literature, art, architecture, and law. The Augustan Age, as it is often called, represents a pinnacle of Roman cultural achievement, with works produced during this period continuing to be celebrated and studied for their artistic and intellectual merit.

Chapter 13: Emperor Tiberius of Rome

Emperor Tiberius, born Tiberius Claudius Nero on November 16, 42 BCE, ruled as the second emperor of Rome from 14 CE to 37 CE. His reign is often overshadowed by the legacies of his predecessor Augustus and his successor Caligula, yet Tiberius' administration was marked by significant achievements and complex challenges. Tiberius' life and reign offer a nuanced view of the early Roman Empire, revealing both the strengths and weaknesses of imperial rule.

Tiberius was born into the Claudian family, one of Rome's oldest patrician lines, to Tiberius Claudius Nero and Livia Drusilla. His early years were marked by the political turmoil of the late Republic, which saw the rise of Julius Caesar and the subsequent power struggles following his assassination. In 38 BCE, when Tiberius was just four years old, his mother divorced his father and married Octavian (later Augustus), aligning Tiberius with Rome's emerging power broker.

Tiberius' stepfather, Augustus, would shape much of his future. Augustus' vision for Rome required capable administrators and military leaders, roles for which Tiberius was groomed from an early age. Tiberius first gained military experience under Augustus' generals and soon proved his capability. His early military career included campaigns in the Alps and the Balkans, where he demonstrated his strategic acumen and leadership skills.

In 11 BCE, Tiberius married Vipsania Agrippina, the daughter of Augustus' close friend and general Marcus Agrippa. This marriage was politically advantageous and produced a son, Drusus Julius Caesar. However, Augustus, intent on consolidating his lineage, forced Tiberius to divorce Vipsania and marry Julia the Elder, Augustus' only biological child. This marriage was unhappy and strained Tiberius' relationship with Augustus.

Despite personal setbacks, Tiberius' military career flourished. He successfully commanded legions in Germania and along the Danube, securing Roman frontiers and suppressing revolts. His campaigns extended Rome's influence and provided stability to its borders, crucial for the empire's security. These military successes earned him significant acclaim and positioned him as a leading figure in Augustus' succession plans.

In 6 BCE, however, Tiberius abruptly retired to the island of Rhodes, seeking to escape the political intrigues and personal unhappiness in Rome. This withdrawal puzzled many and strained his relationship with Augustus. Tiberius remained in self-imposed exile for eight years, returning to Rome only in 2 CE at Augustus' insistence, who needed a reliable heir after the deaths of his grandsons, Gaius and Lucius Caesar.

With his return, Tiberius was formally adopted by Augustus, making him the primary heir. He resumed his political and military duties, effectively acting as co-ruler during the latter years of Augustus' reign. When Augustus died in 14 CE, Tiberius was well-prepared to assume power, though his accession was not without challenges. His path to the throne was paved with Augustus' careful planning, but it also came with the burden of living up to his stepfather's monumental legacy.

Tiberius' reign began with a careful consolidation of power. He faced opposition from various quarters, including the Senate and members of the imperial family. Tiberius was a complex figure, known for his cautious and sometimes enigmatic approach to governance. He maintained the façade of republican traditions, respecting the Senate and adhering to the legal frameworks established by Augustus, yet his rule was essentially autocratic.

One of Tiberius' significant early challenges was the mutiny of the legions in Pannonia and Germania in 14 CE. These legions, discontented with their conditions and seeking better pay and terms, rebelled shortly after Augustus' death. Tiberius sent his son Drusus and his nephew Germanicus to quell the mutinies. Germanicus, a popular and charismatic leader, succeeded in restoring order and reaffirmed loyalty to Tiberius. This incident highlighted the fragility of imperial authority and the importance of military loyalty.

Germanicus' prominence posed a potential threat to Tiberius, though the emperor publicly supported him. In 17 CE, Germanicus was sent to the eastern provinces with broad powers. His untimely death in 19 CE, under suspicious circumstances, sparked rumors of foul play and strained relations between Tiberius and Germanicus' widow, Agrippina the Elder. This event contributed to an atmosphere of mistrust and paranoia that increasingly characterized Tiberius' reign.

Administratively, Tiberius continued many of Augustus' policies, emphasizing efficient governance and fiscal prudence. He maintained a balanced budget and accumulated a substantial surplus in the imperial treasury. Tiberius' financial conservatism was aimed at ensuring the long-term stability of the empire, although it sometimes earned him criticism for stinginess.

Tiberius was also known for his judicial reforms. He was accessible to citizens seeking justice and took a personal interest in legal matters, often presiding over trials himself. His reign saw the development of a more formalized legal bureaucracy, contributing to the long-term stability and effectiveness of Roman law.

Despite these achievements, Tiberius' reign was marred by political purges and accusations of tyranny. His increasing reliance on the Praetorian Prefect Lucius Aelius Sejanus contributed to a climate of fear and suspicion. Sejanus, an ambitious and ruthless figure, gradually accumulated power, orchestrating purges of perceived enemies, including members of the imperial family. The relationship between Tiberius and Sejanus remains a subject of historical debate, with some sources suggesting that Sejanus manipulated Tiberius, while others argue that Tiberius was complicit in Sejanus' actions.

In 26 CE, Tiberius withdrew from Rome, relocating to the island of Capri. This retreat from the capital effectively left the administration in the hands of Sejanus. Tiberius' motivations for this withdrawal are unclear; it could have been driven by a desire for a quieter life away from political intrigue, or a strategic move to distance himself from the increasingly dangerous power struggles in Rome.

Sejanus' downfall in 31 CE was dramatic and swift. His ambitions had grown unchecked, and his influence had become a threat to Tiberius himself. Tiberius, perhaps alerted to Sejanus' schemes, ordered his arrest and execution. The purge that followed swept away Sejanus' supporters and further entrenched Tiberius' reputation for paranoia and cruelty. This period of purges and executions deepened the atmosphere of fear and repression in Rome.

The later years of Tiberius' reign were marked by increasing isolation and detachment from the day-to-day affairs of the empire. His governance relied heavily on a small group of trusted advisors, and his communication with the Senate and other political bodies became sporadic. Despite this, the administrative machinery of the empire continued to function effectively, a testament to the robustness of the structures established by Augustus and maintained by Tiberius.

Tiberius died on March 16, 37 CE, at the age of 77. His death marked the end of a reign that was both successful and controversial. He was succeeded by his grand-nephew Caligula, the son of Germanicus, whose rule would quickly take a dramatically different turn. Tiberius' legacy is complex; he maintained the stability and prosperity of the empire, continued important reforms, and managed the transition of power effectively, yet his reign was also characterized by suspicion, political purges, and a withdrawal from direct governance.

Historically, Tiberius has often been judged harshly, portrayed as a tyrant by ancient sources such as Suetonius and Tacitus. These accounts, written during the reigns of subsequent emperors who had reasons to vilify Tiberius, depict him as a paranoid and cruel ruler, driven by personal vendettas and mistrust. Modern historians, however, offer a more balanced view, recognizing his administrative and military achievements while acknowledging the darker aspects of his rule.

Tiberius' impact on the Roman Empire was significant. He consolidated the gains made by Augustus, ensuring the empire's continued stability and prosperity. His judicial and financial policies contributed to the long-term durability of Roman institutions. Despite the controversies and challenges of his reign, Tiberius left a functioning and stable empire to his successors.

The study of Tiberius' reign provides valuable insights into the complexities of Roman imperial governance. His life and rule reflect the tensions between autocracy and republican traditions, the challenges of succession and legitimacy, and the intricate dynamics of power and personal ambition. Tiberius' ability to navigate these challenges, albeit with significant flaws, underscores the resilience and adaptability of the Roman imperial system.

Chapter 14: Emperor Caligula of Rome

Emperor Caligula, born Gaius Julius Caesar Augustus Germanicus on August 31, 12 CE, ruled as the third Roman emperor from 37 CE until his assassination in 41 CE. His reign is one of the most infamous in Roman history, marked by tales of extravagant excess, cruelty, and madness. While his rule lasted only four years, it left a lasting impression on both contemporary observers and later historians, who have painted a picture of an emperor who descended into tyranny and megalomania.

Caligula was born into a family with a prestigious lineage. He was the son of Germanicus, a popular and successful Roman general, and Agrippina the Elder, who was the granddaughter of Augustus. His early life was spent in the military camps where his father was stationed, and it was here that he acquired the nickname "Caligula," meaning "little boots," due to the miniature military boots he wore as a child. Despite this affectionate nickname, his early years were tumultuous and marked by political intrigue and tragedy.

When Caligula was just seven years old, his father Germanicus died under suspicious circumstances while on a mission in the eastern provinces. Many believed he was poisoned, possibly on the orders of Emperor Tiberius, who may have seen Germanicus as a potential rival. The death of his father led to a series of tragic events for Caligula's family. His mother Agrippina and his brothers Nero and Drusus were accused of treason and subsequently exiled or imprisoned. Caligula himself was spared, but he was effectively held under the watchful eye of Tiberius, who summoned him to the island of Capri in 31 CE.

On Capri, Caligula lived under the direct influence of Tiberius, a period that profoundly impacted his character and future rule. Tiberius was notoriously reclusive and tyrannical in his later years, and Caligula witnessed firsthand the mechanisms of power, including the political purges and executions that Tiberius conducted. Despite the oppressive atmosphere, Caligula managed to survive and even thrive, learning how to navigate the dangerous waters of imperial politics.

When Tiberius died in 37 CE, Caligula was named his successor. Initially, his ascension to the throne was met with widespread enthusiasm. The Roman populace welcomed the young emperor, seeing him as a fresh start after the grim and oppressive final years of Tiberius' reign. Caligula's early actions as emperor were promising. He reversed many of Tiberius' unpopular policies, released political prisoners, and provided lavish games and public spectacles to gain favor with the people.

However, this period of goodwill was short-lived. Within months, Caligula fell severely ill, and his subsequent recovery marked the beginning of a drastic and alarming change in his behavior. Historians debate the exact nature of this illness, with some suggesting it could have been encephalitis, while others speculate on psychological factors. Regardless, Caligula emerged from this illness with a dramatically altered demeanor.

Caligula's reign soon descended into a series of increasingly erratic and despotic actions. He began to exhibit signs of megalomania, famously declaring himself a living god and demanding that he be worshipped as such. He often appeared in public dressed as various gods, including Jupiter, Apollo, and Hercules, and he ordered the construction of temples and statues in his honor. This self-deification alienated many Romans, who viewed such actions as sacrilegious and blasphemous.

One of the most notorious aspects of Caligula's rule was his extravagant spending and lavish lifestyle. He squandered vast sums of money on lavish building projects, banquets, and games. Among his most infamous projects was the construction of a massive floating bridge across the Bay of Baiae, which he reportedly used to stage an elaborate chariot ride dressed as a god. Such extravagant expenditures quickly depleted the imperial treasury, leading to increased taxation and financial strain on the empire.

Caligula's relationships with the Roman Senate and other political elites deteriorated rapidly. He exhibited a profound contempt for the Senate, often humiliating senators and reducing their power and influence. He revived the treason trials that had been a hallmark of Tiberius' reign, using them as a tool to eliminate perceived threats and seize the property of wealthy individuals. This reign of terror created an atmosphere of fear and suspicion, further isolating Caligula from Rome's political establishment.

Perhaps the most shocking stories about Caligula involve his personal behavior and alleged acts of sadism and cruelty. Ancient historians such as Suetonius and Cassius Dio recount numerous tales of his brutality, including claims that he enjoyed watching torture and executions, and that he killed for amusement. He is also said to have indulged in incestuous relationships with his sisters, particularly Drusilla, whom he is believed to have regarded with a quasi-divine reverence.

One of the most bizarre and often-cited anecdotes about Caligula is his appointment of his horse, Incitatus, to the high office of consul. While this story is likely exaggerated, it underscores Caligula's disdain for traditional political norms and his desire to mock the institutions of the Republic. It reflects his increasingly erratic and autocratic rule, which alienated virtually all sectors of Roman society.

Caligula's actions also had serious diplomatic repercussions. His reckless foreign policy decisions and erratic behavior led to tensions with Rome's allies and adversaries alike. He launched a bizarre campaign in Gaul and Britain, which included a farcical attempt to collect seashells as spoils of war. Such antics undermined Rome's military credibility and strained relations with neighboring states.

The tipping point for many was Caligula's increasing paranoia and the series of purges and executions that he ordered against perceived enemies, including members of his own family and close associates. His behavior became increasingly unpredictable, and he surrounded himself with sycophants and loyalists, further isolating himself from reality. The climate of fear and instability created by his rule eventually led to a conspiracy to remove him from power.

On January 24, 41 CE, Caligula was assassinated by members of the Praetorian Guard, led by officers Cassius Chaerea and Cornelius Sabinus. The conspirators also targeted his wife, Caesonia, and their infant daughter, Julia Drusilla, to prevent any potential claims to the throne. Caligula's death marked the end of one of the most tumultuous and controversial reigns in Roman history. He was succeeded by his uncle, Claudius, who restored a degree of stability to the empire.

The legacy of Caligula is one of infamy. Ancient sources, primarily Suetonius, Tacitus, and Cassius Dio, portray him as a tyrant whose reign was marked by cruelty, madness, and extravagance. These accounts, written in the decades following his death, are often sensationalized and reflect the biases of their authors. Modern historians approach these sources with caution, recognizing the need to disentangle fact from propaganda.

Caligula's reign highlights the inherent dangers and instabilities of the Roman imperial system, particularly the concentration of power in a single individual. His rule serves as a cautionary tale about the potential for absolute power to corrupt absolutely, and the importance of checks and balances in governance. Despite the notoriety of his reign, Caligula's life and actions provide valuable insights into the complexities and challenges of ruling one of history's greatest empires.

The psychological and political dynamics of Caligula's rule continue to fascinate historians, psychologists, and political scientists. His reign serves as a case study in the pathology of power, illustrating how personal and psychological factors can profoundly influence the course of history. The stories of his excesses and cruelties, whether wholly accurate or not, underscore the human vulnerabilities at the heart of political power.

Chapter 15: Emperor Nero of Rome

Emperor Nero, born Lucius Domitius Ahenobarbus on December 15, 37 CE, ruled as the fifth Roman emperor from 54 CE until his dramatic downfall and suicide in 68 CE. Nero's reign is one of the most controversial and debated periods in Roman history, characterized by artistic ambition, political machinations, and notorious acts of cruelty and excess. While contemporary sources often vilify him, modern historians have sought to provide a more nuanced understanding of his complex legacy.

Nero was born into a turbulent political environment. His father, Gnaeus Domitius Ahenobarbus, died when Nero was just three years old, leaving his mother, Agrippina the Younger, to navigate the dangerous waters of Roman politics. Agrippina was the sister of Emperor Caligula and the great-granddaughter of Augustus, giving Nero a powerful dynastic connection. After Caligula's assassination in 41 CE, Agrippina married her uncle, Emperor Claudius, in 49 CE, and through her influence, Nero was adopted by Claudius and renamed Nero Claudius Caesar Drusus Germanicus.

Nero's education was entrusted to the philosopher Seneca, who, along with the Praetorian Prefect Sextus Afranius Burrus, became a key advisor during his early reign. These formative years under Seneca's tutelage imbued Nero with a strong interest in arts and culture, which later influenced his personal and political style. When Claudius died—rumored to have been poisoned by Agrippina—in 54 CE, Nero ascended to the throne at the age of 16, becoming the youngest emperor in Roman history at that time.

The early years of Nero's reign, often referred to as the quinquennium Neronis (the first five years of Nero's rule), were marked by relative stability and competent administration, largely due to the guidance of Seneca and Burrus. During this period, Nero focused on public welfare and legal reforms. He reduced taxes, gave aid to cities affected by disasters, and upheld the rights of slaves. His early policies aimed at promoting justice and the well-being of his subjects, earning him popularity among the Roman populace.

However, Nero's relationship with his mother, Agrippina, quickly deteriorated as he sought to assert his independence. Agrippina had played a crucial role in securing his accession and expected to exert considerable influence over his decisions. This power struggle reached a climax when Nero began an affair with Poppaea Sabina, which Agrippina vehemently opposed. In 59 CE, Nero orchestrated his mother's murder, an act that marked the beginning of his descent into tyranny and paranoia. The official version suggested an "accidental" drowning, but later accounts reveal more direct methods of assassination.

Freed from his mother's dominance, Nero's behavior grew increasingly erratic. He indulged his passions for music, theater, and chariot racing, often participating in public performances—acts considered unbecoming for a Roman emperor. His dedication to the arts led to the establishment of the Neronia, a series of games featuring music, poetry, and athletic competitions modeled after the Greek Olympics. Nero's artistic pursuits, while popular with the masses, alienated the senatorial elite, who viewed them as frivolous and beneath the dignity of the imperial office.

Nero's personal life further scandalized Roman society. His marriage to Octavia, the daughter of Claudius, ended in divorce and her subsequent execution on charges of adultery. Nero then married Poppaea, whose influence over him was considerable. Poppaea herself died under mysterious circumstances, reportedly from a kick inflicted by Nero during her pregnancy, although some sources suggest a more natural cause.

The Great Fire of Rome in 64 CE is one of the most infamous events associated with Nero's reign. The fire raged for six days, destroying much of the city. Ancient historians, including Tacitus,

Suetonius, and Cassius Dio, suggest that Nero may have started the fire to clear land for his ambitious urban renewal projects, particularly the construction of his lavish Golden House (Domus Aurea). This sprawling palace featured opulent gardens, an artificial lake, and a colossal statue of Nero himself, embodying his grandiose vision for Rome.

In the aftermath of the fire, Nero sought to deflect blame by accusing the Christians, a small and largely misunderstood religious sect, of arson. This led to the first significant persecution of Christians in Roman history. Nero's actions during this period have been a focal point for historical and theological debate, contributing to his legacy as a tyrant and a persecutor.

Nero's later reign was marked by increasing autocracy and financial extravagance. His building projects and lavish lifestyle drained the imperial treasury, necessitating heavy taxation and the confiscation of properties from wealthy citizens. These measures, along with his erratic behavior and the brutal purges of political rivals, fostered widespread discontent among the Roman elite and the military.

Revolts and conspiracies against Nero began to surface. In 65 CE, the Pisonian conspiracy, led by the senator Gaius Calpurnius Piso, aimed to assassinate Nero and restore the Republic. The plot was discovered, and Nero responded with a brutal crackdown, resulting in the execution of numerous senators, officers, and even his former tutor, Seneca. This purge further isolated Nero from the aristocracy and heightened the atmosphere of fear and mistrust.

Nero's popularity continued to wane as his mismanagement of the empire became more apparent. In 66 CE, a major revolt erupted in Judaea, leading to the First Jewish-Roman War. Nero dispatched his general Vespasian to quell the rebellion, a task that would eventually lead to Vespasian's rise to power. In 68 CE, a series of revolts broke out in the provinces, beginning with the rebellion of Gaius Julius Vindex in Gaul and soon spreading to Spain, where the governor, Servius Sulpicius Galba, declared himself emperor.

Faced with mounting opposition and deserted by his Praetorian Guard, Nero fled Rome. On June 9, 68 CE, cornered and abandoned, he committed suicide with the assistance of his secretary Epaphroditus, famously exclaiming, "Qualis artifex pereo!" ("What an artist dies in me!"). His death marked the end of the Julio-Claudian dynasty and plunged the Roman Empire into a brief period of civil war known as the Year of the Four Emperors.

Nero's legacy is a complex and multifaceted one. Ancient sources, written predominantly by members of the senatorial class who had suffered under his rule, portray him as a cruel and decadent despot. Suetonius' "The Twelve Caesars" and Tacitus' "Annals" depict a ruler consumed by vanity and madness, whose reign was characterized by excessive cruelty, artistic pretensions, and neglect of traditional Roman values.

Modern historians, while acknowledging the biases of these sources, have sought to understand Nero within the broader context of his time. Some argue that his focus on public entertainments and artistic endeavors was an attempt to connect with the common people, contrasting the austere and often oppressive rule of his predecessors. Nero's architectural projects, particularly the rebuilding of Rome after the fire, reflected an ambitious vision for the city's future, despite the financial strain they imposed.

Nero's persecution of Christians, while a minor episode in the context of his reign, had a profound impact on the early Christian community and the development of Christian theology. His actions solidified his place in Christian tradition as a symbol of tyranny and evil, influencing later interpretations of his reign.

In the centuries following his death, Nero's name became synonymous with tyranny and debauchery. The legend of Nero as the archetypal mad emperor has endured in popular culture, influencing literature, art, and historical discourse. Yet, beneath the sensationalism lies a more complex figure—a ruler whose reign was marked by significant cultural contributions and profound political challenges.

69

Chapter 16: Emperor Vespasian of Rome

Emperor Vespasian, born Titus Flavius Vespasianus on November 17, 9 CE, ruled as the Roman emperor from 69 CE until his death in 79 CE. His ascent to power marked the end of the chaotic Year of the Four Emperors and the beginning of the Flavian dynasty. Vespasian's reign was characterized by significant military achievements, fiscal reforms, extensive public works, and efforts to restore stability and order to the Roman Empire after a period of intense civil strife.

Vespasian was born in the small village of Falacrina in the Sabine hills, northeast of Rome. His family was of modest, yet respectable, equestrian status. His father, Titus Flavius Sabinus, was a tax collector and moneylender, while his mother, Vespasia Polla, came from a more distinguished lineage. Vespasian had an older brother, also named Sabinus, who would later become an important political ally.

Vespasian's early career followed the traditional cursus honorum, the sequential order of public offices held by aspiring politicians in the Roman Republic and early Empire. He served as a military tribune in Thrace, a quaestor in Crete and Cyrene, an aedile, and a praetor. His military skills became evident during his service in Germany and Britain. In 43 CE, he played a crucial role in the Roman invasion of Britain under Emperor Claudius, commanding the Second Legion Augusta and contributing significantly to the Roman victories that led to the subjugation of the southern part of the island.

Following his successful military career, Vespasian held the consulship in 51 CE and later served as proconsul of Africa, where he gained a reputation for fairness and administrative competence. However, his fortunes took a downturn under Emperor Nero, when he fell out of favor and was forced into a period of relative obscurity.

Vespasian's return to prominence came during the Jewish Revolt of 66 CE. Nero appointed him to command the Roman legions tasked with quelling the rebellion in Judaea. Vespasian proved to be a capable and ruthless military leader, systematically defeating the Jewish forces and recapturing key territories. By 68 CE, he had largely pacified the region, and his son Titus continued the campaign, culminating in the destruction of Jerusalem in 70 CE.

The year 69 CE, known as the Year of the Four Emperors, was a period of intense civil war and political upheaval following Nero's death. After the short and turbulent reigns of Galba, Otho, and Vitellius, Vespasian was declared emperor by the legions in Egypt and Judaea. He garnered widespread support from the eastern provinces and the Danube legions, ultimately defeating Vitellius's forces and securing his position as emperor.

One of Vespasian's first acts as emperor was to restore stability and order to the Roman Empire. The civil wars had left the state treasury depleted and the economy in disarray. Vespasian implemented a series of fiscal reforms to replenish the imperial coffers, including increasing taxes, revoking certain tax exemptions, and instituting new taxes on public urinals—a measure that led to the famous phrase "pecunia non olet" ("money does not stink"). He also restructured the empire's financial administration to ensure more efficient and honest tax collection.

Vespasian's reign is notable for its extensive public works and construction projects. Perhaps the most famous of these is the Flavian Amphitheatre, better known as the Colosseum. Construction of this iconic structure began in 70 CE and was completed by his son Titus in 80 CE. The Colosseum, capable of seating around 50,000 spectators, was designed to host gladiatorial contests, animal hunts, and other public spectacles, serving as a symbol of Roman engineering prowess and Vespasian's commitment to the Roman people.

In addition to the Colosseum, Vespasian embarked on numerous other building projects aimed at restoring and beautifying Rome. He rebuilt the Capitol, which had been destroyed during the civil wars, and constructed new temples, public baths, and forums. His building program extended beyond Rome to the provinces, where he commissioned the construction of roads, aqueducts, and other infrastructure to facilitate communication and trade across the empire.

Vespasian also made significant efforts to reform the Roman military. He reduced the size of the Praetorian Guard, which had become a powerful and often disruptive political force, and ensured that loyal and competent officers were appointed to key positions. He reorganized the provincial legions, establishing a more stable and disciplined military structure. These reforms helped to secure the frontiers of the empire and maintain peace within its borders.

Vespasian's administrative reforms extended to the Senate and other branches of government. He sought to strengthen the authority and dignity of the Senate by restoring its traditional powers and responsibilities. He also took steps to curtail the corruption and abuses that had become rampant during the later years of the Julio-Claudian dynasty. By promoting capable and loyal individuals to positions of power, Vespasian fostered a more meritocratic and stable governing apparatus.

Despite his many achievements, Vespasian faced several challenges during his reign. One significant threat came from the Batavian Revolt in 69–70 CE, led by the Romanized Batavian chieftain Gaius Julius Civilis. The revolt, which took place in the province of Germania Inferior, posed a serious challenge to Roman authority in the region. Vespasian dispatched his generals to quell the uprising, and by the end of 70 CE, the rebellion was suppressed, and Roman control was reestablished.

Vespasian's relationship with the Roman elite was complex. While he sought to restore traditional Roman values and strengthen the Senate, his rise to power was not without controversy. Some senators resented his relatively humble origins and the manner in which he had come to power. Nonetheless, Vespasian's pragmatic and conciliatory approach won him the support of many influential figures, allowing him to govern effectively and maintain stability.

Throughout his reign, Vespasian was known for his wit and down-to-earth demeanor. Anecdotes about his humor and straightforwardness abound, illustrating a ruler who was accessible and relatable to his subjects. He was also known for his frugality and disdain for the excesses that had characterized the reigns of some of his predecessors. These qualities endeared him to the Roman people and helped to solidify his reputation as a capable and virtuous ruler.

Vespasian's health began to decline in the late 70s CE, and by 79 CE, he fell seriously ill. Despite his condition, he continued to attend to his duties as emperor. According to Suetonius, as he lay on his deathbed, Vespasian famously quipped, "Vae, puto deus fio" ("Oh dear, I think I am becoming a god"), mocking the tradition of deifying emperors after their death. He died on June 23, 79 CE, and was succeeded by his eldest son, Titus.

Vespasian's death marked the beginning of a stable and prosperous period for the Roman Empire. His pragmatic and effective governance had laid the groundwork for the success of the Flavian dynasty, which continued under his sons Titus and Domitian. Vespasian was deified by the Senate after his death, an honor that reflected the high regard in which he was held by many Romans.

The legacy of Vespasian is multifaceted. He is remembered as a military leader who restored stability and order to the Roman Empire after a period of chaos. His fiscal and administrative reforms helped to rejuvenate the imperial finances and establish a more efficient and honest government. His extensive building projects, particularly the construction of the Colosseum, left a lasting mark on the physical and cultural landscape of Rome.

Modern historians view Vespasian as one of Rome's most capable and pragmatic emperors. His reign is often seen as a turning point that brought an end to the excesses and instability of the late Julio-Claudian period and ushered in a new era of relative stability and prosperity. While his methods were sometimes ruthless, his ultimate goals were the restoration and preservation of the Roman state.

Chapter 17: Emperor Trajan of Rome

Emperor Trajan, born Marcus Ulpius Traianus on September 18, 53 CE, is often remembered as one of the greatest Roman emperors. His reign from 98 CE to 117 CE marked a period of extensive military conquests, significant public works, and administrative efficiency, earning him the title of optimus princeps, or "the best ruler." Trajan's leadership not only expanded the Roman Empire to its maximum territorial extent but also left a lasting legacy of infrastructural improvements and social reforms that solidified his place in history as a model emperor.

Trajan was born in Italica, in the Roman province of Hispania Baetica, present-day Spain. He came from a well-established senatorial family with strong military traditions. His father, Marcus Ulpius Traianus, served as a distinguished general and senator under Emperor Vespasian. Trajan's upbringing was steeped in Roman military and political culture, preparing him for a life of public service and leadership.

Trajan's early career was marked by steady progression through the ranks of the Roman military and political hierarchy. He served as a tribune, praetor, and eventually as consul in 91 CE. His military acumen was demonstrated through his command in various campaigns, notably in the provinces of Germania and along the Danube frontier. His successes in these roles earned him a reputation as a capable and reliable leader, garnering the attention and favor of Emperor Nerva.

When Emperor Nerva faced challenges to his authority, he adopted Trajan as his heir in 97 CE, in a move designed to stabilize the empire and ensure a smooth succession. Nerva's choice was widely accepted by both the military and the Senate, highlighting Trajan's broad-based support. Upon Nerva's death in 98 CE, Trajan ascended to the throne without opposition, becoming the first Roman emperor born outside of Italy.

Trajan's reign is distinguished by a series of military campaigns that expanded the Roman Empire to its greatest territorial extent. His first major conquest was Dacia, a region corresponding to modern-day Romania and Moldova. The Dacian Wars (101–102 CE and 105–106 CE) were prompted by the threat posed by King Decebalus, who had previously defeated Roman forces. Trajan's campaigns were meticulously planned and executed, culminating in the defeat of Decebalus and the annexation of Dacia as a Roman province. The victory brought immense wealth to Rome, as the Dacian gold mines provided a significant boost to the imperial treasury.

The conquest of Dacia was commemorated by the construction of Trajan's Column in Rome, an architectural and artistic marvel that stands to this day. The column, which features a spiraling frieze depicting scenes from the Dacian Wars, serves as a testament to Trajan's military achievements and his commitment to public works. It remains one of the most important sources of information about Roman military practices and the emperor's campaigns.

Following the Dacian Wars, Trajan turned his attention to the eastern frontier of the empire. His Parthian campaign (113–117 CE) aimed to subdue the Parthian Empire and secure Roman dominance in the region. Trajan's forces advanced deep into Parthian territory, capturing the capital city of Ctesiphon and annexing parts of Mesopotamia. Although these gains were difficult to maintain and were largely abandoned after his death, the campaign demonstrated Trajan's ambition and military prowess.

In addition to his military conquests, Trajan is renowned for his extensive public works and infrastructural projects. He invested heavily in the construction and restoration of roads, bridges, aqueducts, and public buildings throughout the empire. One of his most significant projects was the construction of the Via Traiana, an extension of the Via Appia that improved connectivity between Rome and the southern provinces of Italy. This road facilitated trade, communication, and military movement, contributing to the economic and strategic stability of the empire.

Trajan also undertook major construction projects within the city of Rome itself. The Forum of Trajan, completed in 113 CE, was a grand complex that included the Basilica Ulpia, a vast open plaza, and the aforementioned Trajan's Column. The forum served as a center for legal and commercial activities, reflecting Trajan's commitment to enhancing the civic infrastructure of the capital. The complex was designed by the famed architect Apollodorus of Damascus, who played a key role in many of Trajan's architectural endeavors.

Another notable project was the construction of the Port of Trajan at Ostia, the principal seaport of Rome. The port was expanded and improved to accommodate the increasing volume of trade and grain shipments essential to feeding the growing population of Rome. This project not only enhanced Rome's logistical capabilities but also underscored Trajan's attention to the economic well-being of his subjects.

Trajan's reign was also marked by significant social and administrative reforms. He sought to address the welfare of the Roman populace through various measures. The Alimenta program, for instance, provided financial assistance to impoverished children in Italy. Funded by a combination of private donations and state resources, the program aimed to ensure that children received proper nutrition and education, thereby fostering a more prosperous and stable society.

Administratively, Trajan worked to streamline the governance of the empire and combat corruption. He appointed capable governors to the provinces, emphasizing merit and competence over political connections. Trajan's letters to Pliny the Younger, who served as governor of Bithynia-Pontus, reveal his hands-on approach to administration and his concern for the efficient and fair management of provincial affairs. These letters provide valuable insights into Trajan's governing philosophy and his efforts to maintain justice and order across the empire.

Trajan's relationship with the Senate was generally positive, as he sought to restore the cooperative spirit that had characterized the early Roman Empire. He respected senatorial privileges and often consulted the Senate on matters of state, fostering a sense of shared governance. This approach helped to stabilize the political landscape and reinforce the legitimacy of his rule.

Religiously, Trajan maintained the traditional Roman pantheon and supported the existing religious institutions. His policies towards Christians, however, were more complex. While he did not actively persecute Christians, he upheld the laws that prohibited the practice of Christianity. His correspondence with Pliny the Younger indicates a pragmatic approach: Christians who were openly defiant were punished, but those who recanted and worshipped the Roman gods were pardoned. This policy reflected Trajan's desire to maintain public order while avoiding unnecessary cruelty.

Trajan's final years were marked by the Parthian campaign, which strained his health and the resources of the empire. In 117 CE, while returning from the campaign, Trajan fell ill and died on August 8 in the city of Selinus in Cilicia (modern-day Turkey). His death marked the end of an era of expansion and consolidation for the Roman Empire.

Trajan's legacy was honored by his successor and adopted son, Hadrian, who ensured that Trajan was deified by the Senate, a common practice for esteemed emperors. Hadrian, while differing in his approach to governance and military policy, continued many of Trajan's administrative and infrastructural reforms, cementing the stability and prosperity of the empire.

In assessing Trajan's legacy, historians often highlight his balanced approach to leadership. His military conquests, particularly in Dacia and the East, demonstrated his strategic acumen and expanded the empire's boundaries. His extensive public works and infrastructural projects improved the quality of life for Roman citizens and showcased the engineering prowess of the era. His social and administrative reforms fostered a sense of justice and efficiency in governance, laying the groundwork for a stable and prosperous society.

Trajan's reign is often seen as the high point of the Roman Empire, a period of territorial expansion, economic prosperity, and cultural achievement. His title of optimus princeps reflects the admiration and respect he garnered during his lifetime and the enduring impact of his rule. Trajan's example set a high standard for subsequent emperors, and his legacy continues to be studied and celebrated as a model of effective and benevolent leadership.

Chapter 18: Emperor Hadrian of Rome

Emperor Hadrian, born Publius Aelius Hadrianus on January 24, 76 CE, ruled as the Roman emperor from 117 CE until his death in 138 CE. He is remembered as one of the "Five Good Emperors" of Rome, a title given to a series of rulers whose reigns were marked by relative peace, stability, and prosperity. Hadrian's tenure is notable for his extensive travels throughout the empire, his architectural and cultural contributions, and his administrative reforms. His reign represents a period of consolidation and cultural flourishing, distinguishing him from his more expansionist predecessors.

Hadrian was born in Italica, in the Roman province of Hispania Baetica, modern-day Spain. He came from a prominent family of senatorial rank, closely related to Emperor Trajan. His father, Publius Aelius Hadrianus Afer, died when Hadrian was ten, and he was subsequently placed under the guardianship of Trajan and Publius Acilius Attianus, who ensured his education and early career in public service. Hadrian's early life was marked by a rigorous education in literature, philosophy, and military training, preparing him for future leadership.

Hadrian's career advanced steadily under the reign of Trajan, to whom he was both a relative and a trusted confidant. He held various military and administrative positions, including serving as a legate in the Dacian Wars and as a governor in Pannonia. His competence and loyalty earned him Trajan's favor, and he was eventually appointed as legate of the prestigious Legio I Minervia. Hadrian also married Trajan's grand-niece, Vibia Sabina, further solidifying his ties to the imperial family.

The circumstances surrounding Hadrian's accession to the throne remain somewhat controversial. Trajan's health declined during his Parthian campaign, and he died in 117 CE without a clear successor. It is widely believed that Trajan's wife, Plotina, played a crucial role in ensuring Hadrian's adoption and succession, possibly even after Trajan's death. Despite these uncertainties, Hadrian was declared emperor by the Senate without significant opposition, marking the beginning of his reign.

Hadrian's approach to governance differed markedly from that of his predecessor. While Trajan had pursued an aggressive policy of territorial expansion, Hadrian focused on consolidating and securing the existing boundaries of the empire. One of his first acts as emperor was to abandon Trajan's conquests in Mesopotamia and Armenia, recognizing the difficulty of maintaining these distant territories. This decision reflected Hadrian's pragmatic approach to empire management, prioritizing stability and defensible borders over expansion.

Hadrian's reign is particularly distinguished by his extensive travels throughout the Roman Empire. Unlike many of his predecessors, who largely remained in Rome, Hadrian spent more than half of his reign traveling to nearly every province. These journeys served multiple purposes: they allowed Hadrian to personally inspect and improve the administration of the provinces, ensure the loyalty of local elites, and oversee military defenses. His presence in the provinces reinforced imperial authority and fostered a sense of unity within the diverse empire.

One of Hadrian's most significant achievements was the construction of Hadrian's Wall in Britain. This defensive fortification, stretching approximately 73 miles from the River Tyne to the Solway Firth, was designed to protect the northern frontier of the Roman province of Britannia from incursions by the Picts and other tribes. The wall was a massive undertaking, involving the construction of forts, milecastles, and turrets along its length. Hadrian's Wall not only served as a military barrier but also as a symbol of Roman power and engineering prowess. It remains one of the most enduring monuments of Roman Britain.

Hadrian's architectural legacy extended far beyond Britain. He was a patron of the arts and a prolific builder, commissioning numerous projects throughout the empire. In Rome, he rebuilt the Pantheon, one of the most iconic and well-preserved structures of ancient Rome. The new Pantheon, completed around 126 CE, featured a massive dome with a central oculus, an engineering marvel that has inspired architects for centuries. The Pantheon's design, with its harmonious proportions and use of light, exemplifies Hadrian's appreciation for both engineering and aesthetics.

Another of Hadrian's notable architectural contributions was his villa at Tivoli, near Rome. This sprawling complex, covering more than 250 acres, served as a retreat and administrative center. The villa incorporated a variety of architectural styles and featured numerous buildings, including theaters, libraries, baths, and temples. It reflected Hadrian's eclectic tastes and his interest in Greek and Egyptian culture, as well as his desire to create a microcosm of the empire. The villa's innovative design and luxurious amenities made it one of the most impressive residential complexes of the ancient world.

Hadrian's travels also took him to Greece, where he developed a deep admiration for Greek culture. He sought to integrate Greek traditions and aesthetics into Roman life, fostering what is often referred to as the "Hellenistic Renaissance." In Athens, he completed the construction of the Temple of Olympian Zeus, a project that had been begun centuries earlier but left unfinished. Hadrian's contributions to the city earned him the title of "Olympian," and he was honored with numerous statues and inscriptions.

In addition to his architectural and cultural initiatives, Hadrian implemented significant administrative reforms aimed at improving the governance of the empire. He reorganized the Roman bureaucracy, creating a more professional and efficient civil service. He also codified Roman law, issuing the Perpetual Edict, which standardized legal procedures and reduced the arbitrary application of justice. These reforms helped to stabilize the empire's administration and ensure more consistent governance across its vast territories.

Hadrian's reign was not without challenges, particularly regarding his relationship with the Roman Senate. His decision to execute four leading senators shortly after his accession created tension and suspicion. While the exact reasons for these executions remain unclear, they were likely motivated by concerns over potential conspiracies against his rule. Despite this rocky start, Hadrian sought to mend relations with the Senate over time, involving them in his reforms and respecting their traditional privileges.

One of the most contentious periods of Hadrian's reign was the Bar Kokhba Revolt in Judea (132–136 CE). The revolt, led by Simon Bar Kokhba, was sparked by Hadrian's decision to rebuild Jerusalem as a Roman colony named Aelia Capitolina and to construct a temple to Jupiter on the site of the Jewish Temple. These actions were seen as deeply offensive by the Jewish population, leading to a widespread and violent uprising. The Roman response was brutal, with extensive military campaigns to suppress the revolt. The conflict resulted in significant casualties and the near-destruction of Judea, as well as severe reprisals against the Jewish people, including a ban on Jewish practices and the renaming of the province to Syria Palaestina.

Hadrian's personal life and relationships also played a notable role in his reign. He was known for his close companionship with Antinous, a young Greek from Bithynia. The nature of their relationship, whether romantic or platonic, has been the subject of much speculation. Antinous accompanied Hadrian on many of his travels, and his untimely death in 130 CE, believed to be by drowning in the Nile, deeply affected the emperor. In his grief, Hadrian deified Antinous, establishing a cult in his honor and founding the city of Antinopolis in Egypt. Statues and coins bearing Antinous's likeness were produced across the empire, reflecting the depth of Hadrian's affection and the widespread influence of the young man's cult.

Hadrian's final years were marked by declining health and preparations for his succession. He adopted Lucius Aelius as his heir, but Aelius's death in 138 CE forced Hadrian to make another choice. He ultimately adopted Antoninus Pius, stipulating that Antoninus in turn adopt Marcus Aurelius and Lucius Verus. This decision ensured a smooth transition of power and the continuation of the stability Hadrian had worked to maintain.

Hadrian died on July 10, 138 CE, at his villa in Baiae, near Naples. His body was initially buried at Puteoli, but his remains were later transferred to Rome and interred in the mausoleum he had constructed for himself, now known as Castel Sant'Angelo. Hadrian was deified by the Senate, a testament to the respect he garnered despite the controversies of his reign.

The legacy of Emperor Hadrian is multifaceted, reflecting his diverse interests and accomplishments. His reign marked a period of consolidation and cultural enrichment, contrasting with the expansionist policies of his predecessors. Hadrian's extensive travels, architectural contributions, and administrative reforms left an indelible mark on the Roman Empire. His efforts to integrate Greek culture into Roman life and his patronage of the arts and architecture fostered a renaissance of classical ideals that influenced subsequent generations.

Hadrian's reign also exemplified the challenges of balancing military, administrative, and cultural priorities within a vast and diverse empire. His pragmatic approach to governance, combined with his personal charisma and vision, established a model of leadership that continued to resonate throughout the Roman world. Despite the difficulties he faced, Hadrian's legacy as a "good emperor" endures, celebrated for his contributions to the stability, prosperity, and cultural flourishing of the Roman Empire.

Chapter 19: Emperor Marcus Aurelius of Rome

Emperor Marcus Aurelius, born Marcus Annius Verus on April 26, 121 CE, is remembered as one of Rome's greatest and most philosophical rulers. His reign from 161 CE until his death in 180 CE was characterized by military conflict, administrative reform, and philosophical reflection. He is often considered the last of the "Five Good Emperors," a term coined by the historian Edward Gibbon to describe the period of stable and benevolent rule from Nerva to Marcus Aurelius. Marcus Aurelius is particularly renowned for his Stoic philosophical work, "Meditations," which continues to be influential to this day.

Marcus Aurelius was born into a prominent and wealthy family in Rome. His father, Marcus Annius Verus, was a Roman senator and his mother, Domitia Lucilla, came from a rich and influential family. His paternal grandfather served as a consul three times, highlighting the family's significant political connections. When his father died when Marcus was just a child, he was adopted by his grandfather, who oversaw his education and upbringing.

From a young age, Marcus was deeply influenced by the teachings of Stoicism, a school of philosophy that emphasized rationality, self-discipline, and virtue. His tutors included the philosopher Junius Rusticus, who introduced him to the works of Epictetus, a former slave whose teachings on Stoic philosophy profoundly shaped Marcus's worldview. These early philosophical influences would remain central to his life and reign.

In 138 CE, Marcus's fortunes changed dramatically when Emperor Hadrian, who had no biological heir, adopted Lucius Ceionius Commodus as his successor. However, when Commodus died unexpectedly, Hadrian then chose Antoninus Pius on the condition that Antoninus adopt Marcus and Commodus's son, Lucius Verus. This decision placed Marcus directly in line for the throne. He was given the name Marcus Aelius Aurelius Verus upon his adoption and became heir apparent.

Under the guidance of Antoninus Pius, Marcus continued his education and began his public career. He held various administrative and military positions, gaining practical experience in governance. In 145 CE, he married Antoninus Pius's daughter, Faustina the Younger, further cementing his ties to the imperial family. The marriage produced 14 children, though many did not survive to adulthood. Their surviving children included Commodus, who would later succeed Marcus as emperor.

When Antoninus Pius died in 161 CE, Marcus Aurelius ascended to the throne alongside his adopted brother Lucius Verus, marking the first time Rome had co-emperors. Although Marcus held the senior position, he shared power with Lucius Verus, a move designed to ensure stability and continuity. This joint rule, however, was soon tested by external threats.

The early years of Marcus's reign were dominated by military challenges. Almost immediately, the Parthian Empire in the east launched an invasion, capturing several Roman territories. Lucius Verus was sent to lead the campaign against the Parthians, while Marcus remained in Rome to manage the administration of the empire. The Parthian War (161–166 CE) was eventually successful, resulting in the sacking of the Parthian capital Ctesiphon and the reassertion of Roman control over the eastern provinces.

However, the return of the Roman legions from the Parthian campaign brought with it a devastating plague, known as the Antonine Plague, which ravaged the empire from 165 to 180 CE. This pandemic, believed to have been either smallpox or measles, caused widespread mortality, significantly reducing the population and weakening the empire's economy and military capabilities.

Concurrent with these challenges, the northern frontiers of the empire came under threat from various Germanic tribes. The Marcomannic Wars (166–180 CE) were a series of conflicts along the Danube frontier, where tribes such as the Marcomanni, Quadi, and Sarmatians launched repeated invasions into Roman territory. These wars required Marcus to spend much of his reign on military campaigns, personally leading his troops and securing the borders. Despite the constant threat of invasion, Marcus managed to achieve several significant victories, although the conflict remained unresolved at the time of his death.

Marcus's dedication to duty extended beyond military matters. His reign was also marked by efforts to reform the administration and improve the welfare of his subjects. He focused on ensuring justice and fairness within the legal system, addressing corruption and inefficiency. His interest in philosophy informed his approach to governance, emphasizing rational decision-making and the welfare of the people.

Despite the pressures of ruling an empire in crisis, Marcus Aurelius found time to pursue his philosophical interests. His "Meditations," written during his military campaigns, is a series of personal reflections and philosophical musings that offer insights into his thoughts and values. Written in Greek, these writings reveal a man deeply committed to the principles of Stoicism, grappling with the challenges of leadership and the transient nature of life. "Meditations" remains a seminal work in the study of Stoic philosophy and is admired for its introspective and practical wisdom.

The personal life of Marcus Aurelius was marked by both joy and tragedy. His marriage to Faustina the Younger was a source of both support and controversy. Historical sources offer mixed accounts of Faustina's character, with some ancient writers accusing her of infidelity and conspiracy. However, these accounts are often considered biased or unreliable. Regardless of the veracity of these claims, Marcus consistently honored Faustina, even after her death in 175 CE, when she was deified and given the title of Augusta.

The question of succession was a significant concern for Marcus Aurelius. Unlike his predecessors who adopted capable adults as heirs, Marcus chose his biological son Commodus, who had been named Caesar and co-emperor in 177 CE. This decision has been widely criticized by historians, as Commodus's subsequent reign (180–192 CE) was marked by erratic behavior and misrule, leading to political instability and contributing to the eventual decline of the Roman Empire. Some speculate that Marcus, aware of his son's flaws, hoped that his guidance and the established administrative systems would help Commodus govern effectively.

In 177 CE, Commodus was made joint emperor, a decision that signaled Marcus's intention for a smooth succession. However, Marcus's health began to decline, exacerbated by the relentless demands of his role and the ongoing military campaigns. He spent his final years on the front lines, continuing to lead his troops against the Germanic tribes. In 180 CE, while at his military headquarters in Vindobona (modern-day Vienna), Marcus Aurelius fell ill and died on March 17.

Marcus Aurelius's death marked the end of the Pax Romana, a period of relative peace and stability that had lasted for over two centuries. His legacy as a philosopher-king, epitomizing the ideals of Stoic virtue and rational governance, has endured through the centuries. The challenges he faced during his reign – from military conflicts and economic difficulties to the devastating plague – tested his leadership and resilience. Despite these trials, his commitment to his principles and the well-being of the empire remained steadfast.

The "Meditations" of Marcus Aurelius offer a unique and intimate glimpse into the mind of a Roman emperor, providing timeless reflections on duty, mortality, and the human condition. His philosophical insights continue to inspire leaders and thinkers, embodying the Stoic ideals of wisdom, courage, and temperance.

Chapter 20: Emperor Constantine the Great

Emperor Constantine the Great, also known as Constantine I, was born Flavius Valerius Constantinus on February 27, 272 CE, in Naissus, present-day Niš in Serbia. He is renowned for being the first Roman emperor to convert to Christianity and for establishing Constantinople (modern-day Istanbul) as the new capital of the Roman Empire. His reign marked a pivotal transformation in the Roman Empire, particularly in the establishment and spread of Christianity. Constantine's policies and actions significantly shaped the future of Europe and the Christian church, leaving a lasting legacy that continued to influence the world for centuries.

Constantine was the son of Flavius Valerius Constantius, a Roman army officer who later became Emperor Constantius I, and Helena, a woman of humble origins who was later venerated as Saint Helena. Constantine's early life was marked by the military and political career of his father, which took the family to various parts of the empire. When his father was elevated to the rank of Caesar, one of the junior emperors, by Emperor Diocletian in 293 CE, Constantine was sent to the court of Diocletian and Galerius in Nicomedia (modern-day İzmit, Turkey), where he received an education in Latin and Greek literature, rhetoric, and philosophy, and gained significant political and military experience.

In 305 CE, after Diocletian and Maximian abdicated, Constantius was promoted to Augustus, the senior emperor of the Western Roman Empire. Constantine joined his father on a military campaign in Britain, but Constantius fell ill and died in 306 CE in Eboracum (modern-day York). Upon his father's death, Constantine's troops proclaimed him Augustus. However, the political landscape of the Roman Empire was complex, with multiple claimants to the throne and a tetrarchic system designed to prevent such power struggles. Constantine's claim was not universally recognized, leading to a series of civil wars and political maneuvers over the next several years.

Constantine's rise to power was marked by a series of military conflicts against rival claimants to the throne, including Maxentius and Licinius. One of the most significant battles in his ascent was the Battle of Milvian Bridge in 312 CE against Maxentius. According to Christian tradition, on the eve of the battle, Constantine experienced a vision of a cross of light in the sky accompanied by the words "In hoc signo vinces" ("In this sign, you will conquer"). That night, he dreamed that Christ instructed him to mark his soldiers' shields with the Christian symbol of the Chi-Rho, an early form of the Christogram. Constantine's subsequent victory at Milvian Bridge, where he defeated and killed Maxentius, marked a turning point in his conversion to Christianity.

In 313 CE, Constantine and Licinius, the ruler of the Eastern Roman Empire, issued the Edict of Milan, which granted religious tolerance throughout the empire and specifically legalized Christianity. This edict ended the persecution of Christians and allowed them to practice their faith openly. The Edict of Milan was a monumental step in the history of Christianity, providing the religion with the freedom to grow and spread more widely within the Roman Empire.

The relationship between Constantine and Licinius eventually deteriorated, leading to a series of conflicts between the two. In 324 CE, Constantine defeated Licinius at the Battle of Chrysopolis, thereby becoming the sole ruler of the Roman Empire. This victory allowed Constantine to further consolidate his power and pursue his vision of a unified and Christianized empire.

One of Constantine's most significant and lasting contributions was the founding of Constantinople as the new capital of the Roman Empire. In 330 CE, he officially dedicated the city, previously known as Byzantium, as Nova Roma (New Rome), although it would come to be known as Constantinople in his honor. The strategic location of the city, on the Bosporus strait connecting Europe and Asia, made it an ideal hub for trade, military defense, and administration. Constantine invested heavily in the city's infrastructure, constructing walls, public buildings, and churches, including the Hagia Sophia, which would become a major center of Christian worship.

Constantinople's establishment marked a shift in the power center of the Roman Empire from Rome in the West to the East. This move had profound implications for the empire's political and cultural future, as the city would later become the capital of the Byzantine Empire, preserving Roman and Christian traditions long after the fall of Rome in the West.

Constantine's reign was also characterized by significant religious and administrative reforms. He convened the First Council of Nicaea in 325 CE, which aimed to address divisions within the Christian Church, particularly the Arian controversy over the nature of Christ. The council produced the Nicene Creed, a statement of faith that affirmed the doctrine of the Trinity and established a foundation for orthodox Christian theology. This council not only sought to unify Christian doctrine but also demonstrated Constantine's commitment to supporting and shaping the Christian Church.

In addition to his religious reforms, Constantine implemented various administrative changes to strengthen and stabilize the empire. He restructured the Roman government, dividing the empire into smaller administrative units called dioceses, each overseen by a vicar. This system improved the efficiency of governance and allowed for better control over the vast territories of the empire. He also reformed the military, creating a more mobile field army to respond to threats more effectively.

Constantine's support for Christianity extended beyond political and administrative measures. He endowed the church with significant wealth and privileges, granting bishops judicial authority and exempting clergy from certain taxes. He also funded the construction of numerous churches, including the Church of the Holy Sepulchre in Jerusalem, which was built on the site believed to be the location of Jesus' crucifixion and resurrection. These actions not only strengthened the church's institutional structure but also facilitated the spread of Christianity throughout the empire.

Despite his many achievements, Constantine's reign was not without controversy and challenges. His relationship with his family was marked by tragedy and conflict. In 326 CE, Constantine ordered the execution of his eldest son, Crispus, and his wife, Fausta, under mysterious circumstances. The reasons behind these executions remain unclear, with some historical accounts suggesting accusations of treason or adultery. These actions cast a shadow over Constantine's legacy and have been the subject of much historical debate.

Constantine's health began to decline in the early 330s, and he spent his final years continuing to govern and support the church. In 337 CE, sensing his end was near, he sought baptism, which he had delayed until then, following a common practice of the time. He was baptized by Eusebius of Nicomedia, a bishop of the Arian faction, which indicates the complex religious landscape and the tensions within early Christianity. Constantine died on May 22, 337 CE, and was buried in the Church of the Holy Apostles in Constantinople, a church he had commissioned.

The legacy of Constantine the Great is profound and multifaceted. His conversion to Christianity and subsequent support for the religion fundamentally altered the course of Western civilization. By legalizing and promoting Christianity, he facilitated its growth from a persecuted sect to the dominant religion of the Roman Empire and later of Europe. His establishment of Constantinople as the new capital ensured the continuation of Roman culture and governance in the East, even as the Western Roman Empire declined.

Constantine's reign also marked significant administrative and military reforms that strengthened the empire and improved its governance. His policies and actions laid the groundwork for the Byzantine Empire, which would preserve and transmit classical knowledge and Christian traditions through the Middle Ages and into the modern era.

Moreover, Constantine's influence on Christian theology and church organization has had lasting impacts. The Nicene Creed, established during his reign, remains a central tenet of Christian faith. His patronage of the church helped to shape its structure and relationship with the state, setting precedents for church-state relations that would endure for centuries.

Chapter 21: Emperor Justinian I of Byzantium

Emperor Justinian I, also known as Justinian the Great, was born in 482 CE in Tauresium, a village in the Roman province of Dardania, which is in present-day North Macedonia. His reign as Byzantine Emperor from 527 to 565 CE was marked by ambitious projects, legal and administrative reforms, military campaigns, and efforts to restore the Roman Empire's former glory. Justinian's legacy is vast, influencing law, architecture, and the structure of the Byzantine Empire, and leaving an indelible mark on the course of history.

Justinian was born Flavius Petrus Sabbatius to a family of modest means. His uncle, Justin I, rose through the ranks of the Byzantine army to become Emperor in 518 CE. Justin adopted Justinian, giving him access to education and the court's resources. Justinian was well-educated, studying theology, law, and Roman history. His rise to power began with his appointment to key military and political positions, where he demonstrated administrative prowess and strategic insight.

Upon the death of his uncle in 527 CE, Justinian ascended to the throne, marking the beginning of a reign characterized by grand ambition and comprehensive reform. One of his most significant contributions was the overhaul of the legal system. Recognizing the chaotic state of Roman law, which had accumulated over centuries, Justinian initiated the creation of the Corpus Juris Civilis, or the Body of Civil Law. This massive legal codification project was directed by the jurist Tribonian and included the Codex Justinianus, Digesta (or Pandects), Institutiones, and Novellae Constitutiones. The Corpus Juris Civilis streamlined and systematized centuries of Roman law, providing a clear and organized legal code. This body of work became the foundation of legal systems in many European countries and influenced legal thought well into the modern era.

Justinian's ambition extended to the religious sphere, where he sought to unify Christianity within the empire and reinforce its dominance. His reign was marked by efforts to combat heresies and consolidate Orthodox Christian doctrine. He played a significant role in the Fifth Ecumenical Council in 553 CE, which aimed to resolve theological disputes and strengthen the unity of the Christian Church. Justinian's religious policies were intertwined with his legal reforms, as he saw the law as a tool to enforce religious orthodoxy and societal order.

In architecture, Justinian's reign saw the construction of some of the most iconic structures of the Byzantine Empire. The most renowned of these is the Hagia Sophia in Constantinople, which was rebuilt after the Nika riots of 532 CE. Designed by the architects Anthemius of Tralles and Isidore of Miletus, the Hagia Sophia was a marvel of engineering and architectural innovation, featuring a massive dome that seemed to float above the central nave. It remained the world's largest cathedral for nearly a thousand years and symbolized the splendor and power of Justinian's reign. Other significant architectural projects included the construction of the Church of San Vitale in Ravenna and the rebuilding of the fortifications along the empire's borders.

Justinian's military campaigns aimed at restoring the Roman Empire to its former territorial extent. He launched extensive and costly wars against the Vandals in North Africa, the Ostrogoths in Italy, and the Visigoths in Spain. His general, Belisarius, achieved remarkable successes, including the reconquest of Carthage in 533 CE and the capture of Rome in 536 CE. These victories temporarily restored significant portions of the Western Roman Empire to Byzantine control, though the campaigns strained the empire's resources and led to prolonged conflict.

The reconquest of Italy was particularly arduous, culminating in the Gothic War (535-554 CE). The war saw multiple sieges of Rome, shifting control between the Byzantines and the Ostrogoths. Despite initial successes, the protracted nature of the conflict devastated the Italian peninsula, leading to economic hardship and depopulation. Ultimately, Justinian's forces regained control of Italy, but the region's infrastructure and economy were severely damaged, and the resources expended contributed to financial strains on the empire.

Justinian's reign was not without significant challenges and controversies. The Nika riots in 532 CE posed one of the most severe internal threats to his rule. Sparked by discontent with his administration and exacerbated by rival factions within Constantinople, the riots led to widespread destruction and chaos in the capital. In a decisive and brutal response, Justinian ordered his generals Belisarius and Mundus to suppress the rebellion, resulting in the massacre of thousands of rioters in the Hippodrome. The suppression of the Nika riots solidified Justinian's power but also demonstrated the precariousness of his position and the potential volatility within the empire.

Another major challenge during Justinian's reign was the outbreak of the Justinianic Plague in 541 CE, a pandemic that swept through the Byzantine Empire and beyond, causing widespread mortality and economic disruption. Believed to be the first recorded instance of bubonic plague, the pandemic killed millions, significantly reducing the population and weakening the empire's economic and military capacities. The plague had long-lasting effects on the empire, contributing to labor shortages, economic decline, and difficulties in sustaining military campaigns.

Throughout his reign, Justinian faced continuous threats from external enemies, particularly the Sassanian Empire to the east. The protracted war with the Sassanians, which lasted from 540 to 562 CE, drained the empire's resources and required constant vigilance. Despite these pressures, Justinian managed to negotiate a "perpetual peace" with the Sassanians in 562 CE, though the stability achieved was temporary.

Empress Theodora, Justinian's wife, played a significant role in his reign, providing counsel and support in both political and religious matters. Theodora, of humble origins, rose to prominence through her marriage to Justinian and was a formidable figure in her own right. She championed social and religious causes, including women's rights and anti-corruption measures, and played a key role in the suppression of the Nika riots. Her influence extended to religious policy, where she supported the Monophysite Christian faction, often putting her at odds with the Chalcedonian Orthodox establishment supported by Justinian.

Justinian's administrative reforms aimed at strengthening the empire's governance and financial stability. He implemented measures to curb corruption and improve the efficiency of tax collection. His administration worked to ensure the stability of the grain supply to Constantinople, a critical factor in maintaining public order and the support of the urban populace. Despite these efforts, the empire faced ongoing fiscal challenges, exacerbated by the costs of military campaigns and the impact of the plague.

Justinian's legal, religious, and military endeavors left a complex legacy. His efforts to codify Roman law provided a lasting foundation for legal systems in Europe and beyond, influencing both civil and common law traditions. His architectural achievements, particularly the Hagia Sophia, stand as enduring symbols of Byzantine splendor and innovation. However, his military campaigns, while initially successful in reclaiming territories, ultimately overextended the empire's resources and contributed to its long-term vulnerability.

Justinian's reign marked the end of an era in many ways. After his death on November 14, 565 CE, the Byzantine Empire faced ongoing challenges, including renewed pressures from external enemies and internal strife. His successors struggled to maintain the territorial gains he had achieved, and the empire gradually transitioned from a Mediterranean-focused power to a more distinctly Eastern entity.

Chapter 22: Empress Wu Zetian of China

Empress Wu Zetian of China, born Wu Zhao in 624 CE, was a remarkable figure in Chinese history. She rose from a concubine to become the only female emperor in more than two millennia of imperial China, reigning from 690 to 705 CE. Her ascent to power, her reign, and her legacy are marked by ambition, political acumen, and significant cultural and administrative contributions, which left an indelible mark on Chinese history.

Wu Zhao was born into a relatively prosperous family. Her father, Wu Shihuo, was a chancellor who served the Tang dynasty, and her mother, Lady Yang, came from a noble family. From a young age, Wu Zhao received an education that was rare for women of her time, learning to read and write, which later played a crucial role in her ability to navigate the complexities of court life and politics.

At the age of fourteen, Wu Zhao entered the court of Emperor Taizong as a concubine, taking the title of cairen, one of the lower ranks of imperial consorts. Her intelligence, beauty, and talent soon caught the emperor's attention. She became a favorite of Taizong, but it was after his death and her subsequent liaison with his successor, Emperor Gaozong, that her rise to power began in earnest. Traditionally, concubines who did not bear the emperor's children were sent to a Buddhist nunnery after the emperor's death. However, Wu Zhao circumvented this tradition by becoming Emperor Gaozong's consort, a maneuver that demonstrated her political astuteness and determination.

Once she became consort to Gaozong, Wu Zhao, now known as Consort Wu, began consolidating power. She bore him several children, which strengthened her position at court. Her most significant political move came in 655 CE when she persuaded Gaozong to depose his wife, Empress Wang, and install her as the new empress. This was a bold and unprecedented move, achieved through a combination of political machinations and ruthless elimination of rivals. Empress Wu's rise to the top was marked by allegations of poisoning, intrigue, and manipulation, reflecting the brutal nature of palace politics.

As empress, Wu Zetian wielded significant influence over Emperor Gaozong, who suffered from chronic illness, which allowed her to manage state affairs. Her role expanded after Gaozong's stroke in 660 CE, when she effectively became the power behind the throne, handling daily administration and making key political decisions. During this period, she began to build a network of loyal officials and ministers, which she used to further consolidate her power.

When Emperor Gaozong died in 683 CE, Wu Zetian became the empress dowager, ruling through her sons who were nominally emperors but effectively figureheads. Her first son, Emperor Zhongzong, attempted to assert his independence, which led to his swift deposition. Wu Zetian then placed her younger son, Emperor Ruizong, on the throne, but continued to wield actual power. By 690 CE, she had amassed enough authority and support to declare herself emperor, founding the Zhou dynasty and becoming the first and only female emperor of China. This bold move was a clear break from Confucian traditions that emphasized male dominance in governance.

As emperor, Wu Zetian implemented numerous reforms aimed at strengthening her rule and improving the efficiency of the government. She expanded the civil service examination system, which recruited officials based on merit rather than birth, thereby reducing the influence of aristocratic families and promoting capable individuals. This system encouraged a more effective and loyal bureaucracy, crucial for the stability and administration of the empire.

Wu Zetian also initiated significant military campaigns to secure and expand China's borders. Her reign saw successful military expeditions against the Tibetan Empire, securing the Tang dynasty's western frontiers. These campaigns demonstrated her ability to maintain and enhance the military strength of her empire, further legitimizing her rule.

In addition to her administrative and military reforms, Wu Zetian was a patron of the arts and Buddhism. She commissioned numerous Buddhist sculptures, temples, and texts, promoting Buddhism as a state religion, which helped to unify the diverse population of the empire under a common spiritual and cultural framework. The Longmen Grottoes, a UNESCO World Heritage site, contains many statues and inscriptions from her era, showcasing her patronage of the arts and religion.

Wu Zetian's reign was also marked by efforts to legitimize her rule through various means. She adopted and promoted the concept of the Mandate of Heaven, which posited that her rise to power was divinely ordained. She also employed a vast network of spies and secret police to root out dissent and eliminate potential rivals, creating an atmosphere of control and surveillance within the court. Her use of political propaganda, such as the discovery of supposed sacred texts predicting a female ruler, further solidified her position and authority.

Despite her achievements, Wu Zetian's reign faced significant challenges and opposition. Traditional Confucian scholars and officials often viewed her rule with suspicion and hostility, given the patriarchal norms of Chinese society. Her methods of eliminating rivals and consolidating power were seen as ruthless, and her heavy reliance on secret police created an atmosphere of fear and intrigue within the court.

Toward the end of her reign, as she aged, Wu Zetian's grip on power began to weaken. She faced increasing resistance from court officials and members of her own family. In 705 CE, a coup led by her son, Li Xian (restored as Emperor Zhongzong), forced her to abdicate the throne. Wu Zetian retired to a secondary palace, where she died later that year. Despite the controversies surrounding her rule, she was buried with full imperial honors in the Qianling Mausoleum, alongside her husband, Emperor Gaozong.

The legacy of Empress Wu Zetian is complex and multifaceted. On one hand, she was a capable and effective ruler who implemented significant reforms that strengthened the central government and promoted cultural and religious development. Her reign challenged the rigid gender norms of her time and demonstrated that a woman could rule as effectively as any man. On the other hand, her methods of securing and maintaining power, including the ruthless elimination of rivals and reliance on secret police, have cast a shadow over her legacy.

Wu Zetian's impact on Chinese history is undeniable. She demonstrated that political acumen and administrative skill could transcend traditional gender roles, leaving a legacy of both controversy and admiration. Her reign contributed to the stability and prosperity of the Tang dynasty, setting a precedent for future generations. In the centuries that followed, her story continued to captivate historians, scholars, and the general public, making her one of the most intriguing and significant figures in Chinese history.

Chapter 23: Emperor Justinian II of Byzantium

Emperor Justinian II of Byzantium, also known as Justinian Rhinotmetos (meaning "the Slit-Nosed"), was one of the most intriguing and turbulent figures in Byzantine history. His reign, spanning two separate periods from 685 to 695 and 705 to 711, was marked by ambitious reforms, fierce military campaigns, a dramatic fall from power, a remarkable comeback, and ultimately, a tragic end. His life story is a testament to the volatile nature of Byzantine politics and the relentless struggle for power.

Justinian II was born in 668 CE, the son of Emperor Constantine IV and Empress Anastasia. As the eldest son, Justinian was groomed for leadership from a young age. He was crowned co-emperor by his father in 681, at the age of 13, ensuring a smooth succession. Constantine IV's reign had been marked by significant military and religious challenges, including the defense against the Umayyad Caliphate and the successful conclusion of the Sixth Ecumenical Council, which resolved the Monothelitism controversy by affirming the doctrine of Dyothelitism.

When Constantine IV died in 685, Justinian II ascended to the throne as a young and energetic ruler. His early reign was ambitious and aggressive, characterized by bold military campaigns and significant administrative reforms. Justinian sought to restore and expand the Byzantine Empire's power, focusing on both internal stability and external threats.

One of his primary military objectives was to secure the empire's eastern frontiers. In 686, he launched a successful campaign against the Umayyad Caliphate, regaining control of parts of Armenia and Iberia (modern-day Georgia). These victories were significant as they temporarily halted the Muslim advance and reasserted Byzantine dominance in the region. Justinian also directed attention to the Balkans, where he launched campaigns against the Slavs and Bulgars, aiming to reassert Byzantine authority over these territories. In 688, he resettled numerous Slavic prisoners in Asia Minor, both to repopulate the area and to use them as a buffer against further Arab incursions.

Domestically, Justinian II was known for his vigorous administrative reforms. He sought to centralize power and improve the efficiency of the imperial government. He implemented tax reforms aimed at increasing state revenue, which, while effective, also increased the burden on the populace, leading to widespread discontent. Justinian's attempts to consolidate power and enforce his reforms often led to conflict with the aristocracy and the church, both of which resented his autocratic style and heavy-handed methods.

Justinian II's reign took a dramatic turn in 695 when his growing unpopularity and harsh measures led to a revolt. The discontent among the aristocracy, military, and general populace culminated in a coup led by the strategos of the Anatolic Theme, Leontios. Justinian was captured, and in a brutal act of mutilation intended to prevent his return to power, his nose was slit—a common practice in Byzantine politics to disqualify someone from ruling. He was then exiled to Cherson, a distant outpost in the Crimea.

While in exile, Justinian displayed remarkable resilience and tenacity. Despite his disfigurement and the seemingly insurmountable odds, he never gave up on reclaiming his throne. During his time in Cherson, he built alliances and bided his time. His opportunity came in 704 when he managed to escape from Cherson and sought refuge with the Khazar Khaganate. There, he married the Khagan's sister, Theodora, securing the Khazar's support.

With the backing of the Khazars, Justinian began plotting his return to power. However, tensions with the Khazar leadership, possibly due to Byzantine bribes or internal politics, forced him to flee once again. This time, he found support from Tervel, the Khan of the

Bulgars, who provided him with an army. In 705, Justinian marched on Constantinople with his Bulgar allies. In a dramatic night-time assault, he managed to retake the city, deposing the then-emperor Tiberios III, who had overthrown Leontios.

Justinian's return to power marked the beginning of his second reign, characterized by a fierce desire for revenge and a determination to reassert his authority. His first act was to exact brutal retribution on those who had wronged him. Leontios and Tiberios III were captured, paraded through the streets of Constantinople, and executed. This display of vengeance was intended to serve as a warning to any potential rivals and solidify Justinian's regained authority.

During his second reign, Justinian continued his ambitious policies, focusing on military campaigns and administrative reforms. He launched another campaign against the Bulgars to reinforce the empire's northern borders and secure alliances. He also resumed efforts to reclaim territories in the east from the Umayyad Caliphate. However, his aggressive policies and autocratic rule once again alienated many within the Byzantine elite and the general populace.

Justinian's second reign was marked by increasing paranoia and a series of purges against perceived enemies and conspirators. His oppressive measures led to widespread discontent and instability. In 711, another revolt broke out, this time led by the strategos of the Theme of Cherson, Bardanes (who later took the name Philippikos). Justinian was overthrown, captured while attempting to flee, and executed, bringing an end to his tumultuous rule.

The legacy of Justinian II is complex and multifaceted. On one hand, he was a capable and ambitious ruler who sought to restore the Byzantine Empire's former glory through military campaigns and administrative reforms. His resilience and determination, particularly his dramatic return to power, demonstrate a remarkable degree of tenacity and political acumen. On the other hand, his autocratic style, harsh measures, and ruthless retribution against his enemies led to widespread resentment and ultimately his downfall.

Justinian II's reign is a reflection of the volatile and often brutal nature of Byzantine politics, where power struggles, coups, and assassinations were commonplace. His life story, marked by dramatic rises and falls, underscores the challenges of maintaining authority in an empire fraught with internal and external threats. Despite his tragic end, Justinian II remains a significant figure in Byzantine history, illustrating both the potential for ambition and the dangers of despotism in the ancient world.

Chapter 24: Charlemagne

Charlemagne, also known as Charles the Great, was born on April 2, 742 (though some sources suggest 747) in what is now Belgium. He was the son of Pepin the Short, King of the Franks, and Bertrada of Laon. Charlemagne's reign, from 768 to 814, marked a turning point in European history, leading to the Carolingian Renaissance and laying the foundations for the future Holy Roman Empire. His life and rule are characterized by vast military conquests, extensive administrative reforms, and a profound cultural revival that had a lasting impact on the history of Europe.

Charlemagne inherited the Frankish throne in 768 upon the death of his father, Pepin the Short, initially sharing power with his brother Carloman. The division of the kingdom was uneasy, marked by rivalry and tension. When Carloman suddenly died in 771, Charlemagne became the sole ruler of the Frankish Kingdom. This consolidation of power allowed Charlemagne to embark on a series of military campaigns that would expand his realm and influence across much of Western Europe.

One of Charlemagne's earliest and most significant military endeavors was the conquest of the Lombard Kingdom in Italy. In 774, responding to a plea for help from Pope Adrian I, who was threatened by the Lombard King Desiderius, Charlemagne marched into Italy. He defeated the Lombards, captured their king, and took the title King of the Lombards. This victory not only expanded his territory but also strengthened his alliance with the Papacy, which would prove crucial for his later endeavors.

Charlemagne's most protracted and challenging campaign was against the Saxons, a pagan Germanic tribe. Beginning in 772, these wars spanned over three decades and were marked by fierce resistance and brutal reprisals. Charlemagne's efforts to subdue the Saxons were not just military but also religious. He aimed to convert them to

Christianity, often employing forceful measures such as the mass execution of Saxon leaders at Verden in 782. The integration of the Saxons into his empire was a testament to his determination and military prowess, though it came at the cost of considerable bloodshed.

In addition to his campaigns in Italy and against the Saxons, Charlemagne also expanded his empire through numerous other military ventures. He subdued the Avars, a nomadic tribe from Central Europe, securing vast amounts of plunder and extending his influence into the Danube basin. His campaigns against the Moors in Spain led to the establishment of the Spanish March, a buffer zone aimed at protecting the Frankish Kingdom from Muslim incursions. Although his attempt to capture Zaragoza in 778 was unsuccessful and led to the famous Battle of Roncevaux Pass, where his rearguard, including the legendary Roland, was ambushed, the campaign demonstrated Charlemagne's far-reaching ambitions.

Charlemagne's conquests laid the foundation for his imperial aspirations. In 800, during a visit to Rome to support Pope Leo III, who had been accused of various crimes and faced rebellion, Charlemagne was crowned Emperor of the Romans on Christmas Day. This coronation by the Pope symbolized the fusion of Roman, Christian, and Germanic elements, heralding the revival of the Western Roman Empire. Charlemagne's new title was not merely ceremonial; it marked the beginning of what would become known as the Holy Roman Empire, a political entity that sought to revive the glory of ancient Rome under a Christian framework.

The title of Emperor brought with it new responsibilities and challenges. Charlemagne took his role as protector of Christendom seriously, engaging in diplomatic and military efforts to safeguard and expand Christian territories. He corresponded with other contemporary rulers, including the Byzantine Empress Irene and the Abbasid Caliph Harun al-Rashid. His diplomatic relations with the latter resulted in the exchange of gifts, including the famous elephant Abul-Abbas, which underscored the reach and influence of his empire.

Charlemagne's reign was not solely defined by his military exploits and imperial ambitions; he was also a great reformer and patron of the arts. His rule ushered in the Carolingian Renaissance, a revival of art, culture, and learning based on classical models. Charlemagne recognized the importance of education and literacy for the administration of his vast empire. He established a palace school at Aachen, his capital, and invited scholars from all over Europe, including the Anglo-Saxon monk Alcuin of York, to teach and produce manuscripts. This intellectual revival led to the preservation and copying of many classical texts, which might have otherwise been lost.

Charlemagne also implemented significant administrative reforms to ensure the efficient governance of his empire. He divided his territory into counties, each governed by a count who was responsible for justice, military defense, and administration. To oversee these counts and ensure their loyalty, he appointed royal agents known as missi dominici, who traveled throughout the empire to enforce the emperor's policies and report on local conditions. This system helped maintain central control over a vast and diverse empire.

One of Charlemagne's notable administrative reforms was the standardization of weights and measures, which facilitated trade and commerce across his empire. He also reformed the monetary system, issuing a new silver coinage that became the standard currency. These economic reforms helped stabilize and stimulate the economy, fostering greater prosperity and integration within his realm.

Charlemagne's reign also had a profound impact on the Church. He viewed himself as a leader of Christendom and took an active role in church affairs. He convened synods and councils to address theological disputes and enforce ecclesiastical discipline. His influence extended to the appointment of bishops and abbots, ensuring that they were loyal to him and capable administrators. This close relationship between the church and state under Charlemagne laid the groundwork for the medieval European notion of a Christian empire.

Despite his many achievements, Charlemagne's reign was not without challenges and controversies. His wars, particularly against the Saxons, were marked by brutality and forced conversions, which have been criticized by historians. The centralized control he sought to impose sometimes led to resistance and rebellion among local rulers and nobility. Additionally, his relationship with the Byzantine Empire was complex and sometimes strained, as the Byzantines did not initially recognize his imperial title.

Charlemagne's legacy was further complicated by the issue of succession. Following Frankish tradition, his empire was divided among his sons. His only surviving legitimate son, Louis the Pious, inherited the empire upon Charlemagne's death in 814. However, the subsequent division of the empire among Louis's sons after his death led to internal conflict and fragmentation, which weakened the Carolingian Empire and eventually contributed to its decline.

Charlemagne died on January 28, 814, and was buried in the Aachen Cathedral, a building he had commissioned and which remains one of his most enduring architectural legacies. His death marked the end of an era, but his influence endured. Charlemagne was later canonized by the church, and his reign became a model for medieval European rulers. The idea of a united Christian Europe under a single emperor continued to inspire political and religious leaders for centuries.

Charlemagne's impact on European history is immense. His reign marked the beginning of the Carolingian Renaissance, which preserved and revived classical knowledge and laid the foundations for the intellectual and cultural developments of the High Middle Ages. His administrative and economic reforms contributed to the stability and prosperity of his empire. As a military leader, he expanded the Frankish kingdom into an empire that encompassed much of Western Europe, shaping the political landscape of the continent.

Moreover, Charlemagne's legacy as a unifier of Europe under Christian rule influenced the development of the Holy Roman Empire and the notion of Christendom. His coronation as Emperor by the Pope symbolized the enduring connection between the church and state in medieval Europe, a relationship that would have profound implications for European history.

Chapter 25: King Alfred the Great of Wessex

King Alfred the Great of Wessex, born in 849 and ruling from 871 to 899, is one of the most renowned figures in English history. His legacy as a wise and just ruler, military strategist, and cultural patron has earned him the epithet "the Great." Alfred's life and reign were marked by his efforts to defend his kingdom against Viking invasions, his significant contributions to law and education, and his role in laying the foundations for the unification of England.

Alfred was born in Wantage, in present-day Oxfordshire, the youngest son of King Æthelwulf of Wessex and his wife Osburh. Despite his royal birth, Alfred's early years were fraught with challenges. The Viking threat loomed large over the Anglo-Saxon kingdoms, and the stability of Wessex was constantly under threat. Alfred's education was also somewhat neglected until his teenage years, but he showed an early interest in learning, which would later manifest in his efforts to promote education and literacy in his kingdom.

Alfred's early experience with Viking warfare began in his youth. His father, King Æthelwulf, had arranged a pilgrimage to Rome with Alfred when he was a child, during which Alfred met the Pope and was anointed as a future king. This trip also exposed Alfred to the wider Christian world and its learning. Upon their return, Wessex faced increased Viking incursions, culminating in the Battle of Aclea in 851, where Alfred's elder brothers successfully repelled a major Viking force. These experiences likely shaped Alfred's understanding of the military and political complexities he would later face as king.

Alfred became king of Wessex in 871 following the death of his brother, King Æthelred I, amidst the ongoing Viking invasions. His accession came at a time of great crisis. The Vikings had already established control over large parts of England, including

Northumbria, East Anglia, and parts of Mercia. The kingdom of Wessex was the last significant Anglo-Saxon stronghold. Alfred immediately faced immense pressure to defend his realm from these formidable foes.

One of Alfred's most significant military achievements was his strategic defense against the Vikings. Early in his reign, he suffered several defeats, but he learned from these setbacks. In 878, Alfred famously retreated to the marshes of Athelney in Somerset after a surprise Viking attack. From this seemingly desperate position, he rallied his forces, gathered intelligence on Viking movements, and prepared a counter-attack. His decisive victory at the Battle of Edington in 878 marked a turning point in his reign. Alfred's forces defeated the Viking army led by Guthrum, who subsequently agreed to the Treaty of Wedmore, converting to Christianity and withdrawing to East Anglia. This treaty not only secured Wessex but also established a period of relative peace and stability.

To prevent future invasions and enhance the kingdom's defenses, Alfred initiated a series of military and infrastructural reforms. He reorganized the military structure of Wessex, creating a network of fortified towns known as burhs. These burhs were strategically located to provide defense and facilitate rapid military response to Viking incursions. Each burh was manned by a local militia, ensuring that every part of the kingdom could be defended quickly. This system of burhs not only enhanced the kingdom's security but also stimulated local economies and encouraged urban development.

Alfred also built a navy to counter the Viking threat from the sea, recognizing the importance of naval power in defending the coastlines. His fleet, though initially small, was innovative and designed to combat the Viking longships effectively. These measures collectively strengthened the kingdom's defenses and deterred further Viking invasions.

Beyond his military accomplishments, Alfred is celebrated for his contributions to education, law, and culture. He was deeply concerned with the moral and intellectual decline of his kingdom, which he believed was partly due to the lack of education and learning. To address this, Alfred embarked on a cultural renaissance, promoting literacy and education among his people. He invited scholars from across Europe to his court, including Asser, a Welsh monk who later wrote a biography of Alfred, providing a valuable contemporary account of his reign.

Alfred's commitment to education led to the establishment of schools and the promotion of literacy in English, rather than Latin, making learning more accessible to the broader population. He commissioned the translation of important religious and philosophical texts into Old English, including Pope Gregory the Great's "Pastoral Care," Boethius's "Consolation of Philosophy," and the first fifty Psalms. These translations helped preserve and disseminate knowledge throughout his kingdom.

In addition to his educational reforms, Alfred is credited with significant legal and administrative contributions. He sought to codify and reform the laws of his kingdom, creating what is now known as Alfred's Law Code. This code was a compilation of earlier Anglo-Saxon laws, combined with Alfred's own statutes and the Ten Commandments. It emphasized justice, fairness, and the protection of the weak, reflecting Alfred's Christian principles. The preface of the law code highlighted Alfred's belief in the king's duty to provide justice and protect his subjects.

Alfred's administrative reforms also included efforts to improve the efficiency of governance. He divided the kingdom into shires and hundreds, creating a more organized and manageable system of local government. This structure facilitated better administration and justice, laying the groundwork for the development of the English common law system.

Alfred's reign was also marked by efforts to foster a sense of unity and identity among the Anglo-Saxon kingdoms. He envisioned a united England and worked towards closer ties with other Anglo-Saxon rulers. His marriage to Ealhswith, a member of the Mercian royal family, strengthened alliances with Mercia. He also maintained diplomatic relations with other European rulers, including the Carolingian Empire, seeking to position Wessex as a significant player in European politics.

Despite his many achievements, Alfred's reign was not without challenges. The threat of Viking raids persisted, and maintaining the loyalty of his nobles and subjects required constant vigilance. However, Alfred's leadership, strategic acumen, and vision for his kingdom enabled him to overcome these challenges and secure a legacy as one of England's greatest kings.

Alfred the Great's legacy extends beyond his death in 899. He is remembered not only for his military and administrative achievements but also for his contributions to education, law, and culture. His vision for a united and educated kingdom laid the foundations for the eventual unification of England under his descendants. Alfred's commitment to justice, learning, and the well-being of his people set a standard for future English monarchs.

Alfred's life and reign have been the subject of numerous historical works, literary adaptations, and cultural references. His character and achievements have inspired generations, and he remains a symbol of resilience, wisdom, and leadership. The enduring respect for Alfred the Great is evident in his depiction in various media, including literature, films, and television, where he is often portrayed as a wise and noble ruler who defended his people and promoted the greater good.

Chapter 26: Genghis Khan

Genghis Khan, born Temüjin circa 1162, is one of history's most formidable conquerors. He founded the Mongol Empire, which became the largest contiguous empire in history after his death. His life, from his early struggles to his ascension as the Great Khan, and his legacy, marked by both unparalleled military successes and significant cultural and administrative achievements, makes him a pivotal figure in world history.

Temüjin's early life was harsh and tumultuous, shaped by the brutal realities of the Mongolian steppes. He was born into the Borjigin clan, a prominent Mongol family. His father, Yesügei, was a chieftain who named his son after a Tatar chieftain he had recently captured. Temüjin's early years were marked by significant upheaval. When he was around nine years old, his father was poisoned by the Tatars, leaving his family vulnerable and destitute. His clan abandoned his family, leaving them to fend for themselves in the harsh Mongolian environment. This early experience of betrayal and hardship profoundly influenced Temüjin's character and future policies.

As a young man, Temüjin faced numerous challenges, including being captured and enslaved by a rival clan. However, he managed to escape and gradually began to build a following. His charisma, strategic acumen, and ability to forge alliances with other Mongol tribes were critical to his rise. He formed a powerful bond with Jamukha, a blood brother or anda, although their relationship would later become strained and lead to conflict.

The key turning point in Temüjin's life came in the early 1200s when he began consolidating various Mongol tribes under his leadership. He employed a combination of military prowess, strategic marriages, and shrewd alliances. One of his significant alliances was with Toghrul, the leader of the Kerait tribe, who acted as a mentor and supporter. However, as Temüjin's power grew, so did the tensions with his allies. Conflicts with Jamukha and Toghrul ultimately led to their downfall and further solidified Temüjin's control over the Mongol tribes.

In 1206, after a series of successful campaigns and strategic victories, Temüjin was proclaimed Genghis Khan, meaning "universal ruler," at a kurultai (a grand assembly of Mongol chiefs). This marked the formal beginning of the Mongol Empire. Genghis Khan's leadership style was revolutionary; he restructured Mongol society and military organization, implementing meritocratic principles that promoted leaders based on ability rather than noble birth. This meritocracy, combined with his innovative military tactics and the unparalleled mobility of his cavalry, made the Mongol army a formidable force.

One of Genghis Khan's first major campaigns was against the Western Xia Dynasty of China. This campaign, which began in 1209, was marked by the Mongols' effective use of psychological warfare and their ability to adapt to different forms of combat. The Western Xia eventually submitted to Mongol rule, paying tribute to Genghis Khan. This victory was followed by the conquest of the Jin Dynasty in northern China, which began in 1211 and culminated in the capture of the Jin capital, Zhongdu (modern-day Beijing), in 1215. These victories not only expanded Genghis Khan's empire but also demonstrated his ability to integrate conquered peoples and their technologies into his military machine.

Genghis Khan's most significant and ambitious campaign, however, was against the Khwarazmian Empire, which spanned present-day Iran, Turkmenistan, Uzbekistan, and Kazakhstan. This campaign was initiated in 1219 after the Khwarazmian ruler, Shah Ala ad-Din Muhammad, executed Mongol envoys, a grave insult that Genghis Khan could not tolerate. The Mongol response was swift and brutal. Genghis Khan's army swept through the Khwarazmian Empire, employing devastating siege tactics and psychological warfare. Cities that resisted were often destroyed, while those that submitted were spared, albeit often heavily taxed. The fall of the Khwarazmian Empire marked the beginning of the Mongol expansion into the Islamic world and demonstrated the terrifying effectiveness of Genghis Khan's military strategy.

Genghis Khan's empire was not only built on military conquest but also on astute governance. He established a legal code known as the Yassa, which codified various aspects of Mongol life, including laws on theft, adultery, and military discipline. The Yassa was a tool for maintaining order and unity within the diverse empire. Genghis Khan also promoted trade and communication across his empire, creating the foundations for what would become the Silk Road. This trade network facilitated cultural and economic exchanges between East and West, significantly influencing the course of world history.

Another notable aspect of Genghis Khan's rule was his religious tolerance. Unlike many contemporary rulers, Genghis Khan allowed his subjects to practice their religions freely. He recognized the strategic advantage of supporting a plurality of faiths, which helped to pacify and integrate the diverse peoples within his empire. This policy of religious tolerance contributed to the stability and cohesion of the Mongol Empire.

Genghis Khan's administrative genius extended to his system of governance. He created a centralized bureaucracy to oversee the vast empire, appointing loyal and capable officials to key positions. He divided his empire into various administrative units, each governed by a trusted general or family member. This system allowed for efficient control and administration over the vast and culturally diverse territories under his rule.

Despite his numerous achievements, Genghis Khan's reign was marked by immense brutality. His military campaigns often involved mass slaughter and destruction. Cities that resisted were often subjected to severe reprisals, including the massacre of entire populations. These tactics, while effective in instilling fear and ensuring compliance, left a legacy of terror and destruction that is still remembered today.

In 1227, during a campaign against the Western Xia, Genghis Khan died under circumstances that remain somewhat mysterious. Some accounts suggest he fell from his horse, while others hint at illness or injury sustained in battle. His death marked the end of an era, but his legacy continued through his successors. Genghis Khan had divided his empire among his four sons, who continued to expand the Mongol territories. The empire eventually stretched from the Sea of Japan to the borders of Eastern Europe, encompassing much of Asia and parts of Europe.

The impact of Genghis Khan's conquests and the Mongol Empire on world history cannot be overstated. The Mongol Empire facilitated unprecedented cultural and economic exchanges across Eurasia. The Silk Road, under Mongol protection, became a major conduit for trade, ideas, and technologies between East and West. This era of relative peace and stability, known as the Pax Mongolica, enabled the transfer of knowledge, goods, and innovations across vast distances.

Genghis Khan's legacy is complex and multifaceted. In Mongolia, he is revered as a national hero and the founder of the Mongol nation. His image adorns currency, monuments, and even vodka bottles, symbolizing national pride and identity. However, in many of the regions he conquered, he is remembered as a ruthless and destructive invader. The dichotomy of Genghis Khan as both a visionary leader and a brutal conqueror reflects the dual nature of his legacy.

In recent years, historians have reevaluated Genghis Khan's contributions to world history, recognizing not only his military prowess but also his impact on global trade, communication, and cultural exchange. His promotion of meritocracy and religious tolerance, as well as his administrative innovations, have been highlighted as significant achievements. Genghis Khan's ability to unite the disparate Mongol tribes and create a cohesive and powerful empire remains a testament to his extraordinary leadership skills.

Chapter 27: King Richard the Lionheart of England

King Richard I of England, known as Richard the Lionheart, was born on September 8, 1157, in Beaumont Palace, Oxford, to King Henry II and Eleanor of Aquitaine. His reign as King of England from 1189 to 1199, though relatively short, was marked by his extraordinary military prowess, his role in the Third Crusade, and his enduring legacy as a chivalric hero. Richard's life and reign were characterized by his martial skills, his complex relationship with his family, and his relentless pursuit of honor and glory.

Richard was the third of five sons born to Henry II and Eleanor, both of whom were formidable figures in their own right. Henry II was the first Plantagenet king of England, establishing a dynasty that would rule for over three centuries. Eleanor of Aquitaine, one of the most powerful and influential women of the medieval period, brought with her the vast and wealthy territories of Aquitaine, significantly bolstering Henry's power. Richard's upbringing was heavily influenced by his mother's court, which was a center of chivalric culture and troubadour poetry.

From an early age, Richard displayed a keen interest in martial activities and knightly pursuits. He was educated in the arts of war and governance, receiving training befitting a prince. Unlike his brothers, Richard quickly earned a reputation for his bravery, military skill, and commanding presence. His mother, Eleanor, played a crucial role in shaping his character, instilling in him the ideals of chivalry and the importance of loyalty and honor.

The Plantagenet family was notoriously fractious, and Richard's relationships with his father and brothers were complex and often contentious. Henry II's attempts to control his vast empire led to frequent conflicts with his sons. In 1173, Richard joined his brothers

Henry the Young King and Geoffrey in a rebellion against their father, encouraged by Eleanor. The rebellion was ultimately unsuccessful, and Richard was forced to submit to his father. However, the tensions within the family persisted.

Richard's primary focus during his youth was the duchy of Aquitaine, which he ruled from 1172. As Duke of Aquitaine, Richard faced numerous revolts from his rebellious vassals. His campaigns to subdue these rebellions were marked by both ruthless efficiency and moments of chivalric largesse. His reputation as a formidable military leader grew during this period, and he earned the respect and loyalty of his subjects in Aquitaine, despite his often harsh methods.

In 1183, the death of his elder brother Henry the Young King made Richard the primary heir to the English throne. However, his relationship with his father remained strained. Henry II's attempts to curtail Richard's power in Aquitaine only fueled further discord. By 1189, the conflict between father and son had reached its peak. Richard allied with Philip II of France, his father's long-time adversary, and launched a campaign against Henry. The aging king was ultimately forced to surrender and name Richard as his heir. Henry II died shortly thereafter, and Richard ascended to the throne of England on July 6, 1189.

Richard's coronation was a grand affair, reflecting his status as a warrior king. However, his attention soon turned to the Holy Land. The fall of Jerusalem to Saladin in 1187 had shocked the Christian world and prompted a call for a new crusade. Richard, deeply pious and eager to prove his chivalric credentials, took the cross and committed himself to the Third Crusade. His preparations for the crusade were extensive and costly, involving the sale of lands and titles to raise funds.

Richard departed for the Holy Land in 1190, accompanied by a large and well-equipped army. His journey to the East was marked by various diplomatic and military maneuvers. He formed an alliance with Philip II of France, although their relationship was fraught with tension and rivalry. Richard's first major action was the capture of the island of Cyprus in 1191, which he secured after a swift and decisive campaign. Cyprus would later prove to be a valuable strategic base for the crusaders.

Richard arrived in the Holy Land in June 1191, where he joined the siege of Acre, a key port city held by Muslim forces. The siege had been ongoing for nearly two years, and Richard's arrival reinvigorated the Christian efforts. His military acumen and leadership played a crucial role in the eventual capture of Acre in July 1191. However, the fall of Acre was accompanied by a notorious massacre of Muslim prisoners, an act that has been the subject of much historical debate and criticism.

Richard's main objective in the Holy Land was to recapture Jerusalem, but this proved to be an elusive goal. Despite his successes on the battlefield, including the decisive Battle of Arsuf in September 1191, logistical and strategic challenges prevented him from advancing on the holy city. Richard's forces were continually harassed by Saladin's troops, and the crusaders struggled with supply issues and internal divisions. Richard and Saladin, though adversaries, developed a mutual respect for each other's military capabilities and chivalric conduct.

The Third Crusade ultimately ended in a stalemate. In September 1192, Richard negotiated a truce with Saladin, known as the Treaty of Jaffa. The treaty allowed Christian pilgrims access to Jerusalem while maintaining Muslim control of the city. Although Richard did not achieve his ultimate goal, his leadership and military prowess had restored Christian territories along the coast and secured safe passage for pilgrims. His actions in the Holy Land solidified his reputation as a great military leader and a paragon of chivalric ideals.

Richard's return journey to England was fraught with peril. In December 1192, while traveling through Europe in disguise, he was captured by Leopold V, Duke of Austria, who held a grudge against Richard for a perceived insult during the crusade. Richard was handed over to Holy Roman Emperor Henry VI and imprisoned, a situation that caused a significant political crisis in England. His mother, Eleanor of Aquitaine, played a crucial role in securing his release by raising a substantial ransom, equivalent to two to three years' income for the English crown. Richard was finally released in February 1194.

Upon his return to England, Richard faced the task of reestablishing his authority and dealing with the political fallout from his absence. His younger brother, John, had attempted to seize power in his absence, allying with King Philip II of France. Richard's response was swift and decisive. He pardoned John, perhaps recognizing the need for family unity, and turned his attention to reclaiming territories lost to the French. The latter years of Richard's reign were dominated by his ongoing conflict with Philip II, known as the Angevin-French War.

Richard's military campaigns in France were marked by a series of sieges and battles as he sought to defend his possessions in Normandy and Aquitaine. Despite his relentless efforts, the war took a heavy toll on both his finances and his health. Richard's indomitable spirit and tactical genius were evident in his ability to hold his own against Philip, a shrewd and capable adversary. However, the conflict remained unresolved at the time of Richard's death.

On March 25, 1199, while besieging the castle of Châlus-Chabrol in Limousin, Richard was struck by a crossbow bolt. The wound became gangrenous, and despite the efforts of his physicians, Richard succumbed to his injuries on April 6, 1199. His death marked the end of an era and left a legacy that would shape English and European history for centuries to come.

Richard the Lionheart's legacy is multifaceted. He is often celebrated as the quintessential knight, embodying the ideals of chivalry, bravery, and honor. His military exploits, particularly during the Third Crusade, earned him a lasting reputation as one of the greatest warrior kings of the medieval period. His skills as a leader and tactician were unparalleled, and his ability to inspire loyalty and admiration among his followers was a testament to his charismatic personality.

However, Richard's reign was not without its controversies and criticisms. His near-constant absence from England, coupled with the heavy taxation required to fund his crusades and wars, placed a significant burden on his subjects. His focus on martial glory often came at the expense of domestic governance, and his kingdom faced significant challenges in his absence. Furthermore, his ruthless treatment of enemies and his involvement in the massacre of prisoners at Acre have marred his legacy with a darker, more brutal image.

Despite these complexities, Richard the Lionheart remains a legendary figure in both history and popular culture. His life has been the subject of numerous historical works, literary adaptations, and artistic representations. The legends surrounding his bravery, his battles, and his enigmatic personality continue to capture the imagination of people around the world. His tomb at the Abbey of Fontevraud in France, where he lies beside his father Henry II and his mother Eleanor of Aquitaine, remains a site of historical and cultural significance.

Chapter 28: King Henry II of England

King Henry II of England, born on March 5, 1133, in Le Mans, France, was a pivotal figure in English history. His reign from 1154 to 1189 marked the beginning of the Plantagenet dynasty and laid the foundations for the English legal system. Henry's life was characterized by his ambitious attempts to consolidate and expand his territories, his turbulent relationships with his family, and his efforts to reform the governance of his kingdom.

Henry was the son of Geoffrey Plantagenet, Count of Anjou, and Matilda, daughter of King Henry I of England. His early life was shaped by his mother's struggle to claim the English throne, which had been usurped by her cousin, Stephen of Blois, after the death of Henry I in 1135. This period of civil war, known as The Anarchy, was marked by widespread unrest and conflict. Henry's upbringing in this tumultuous environment fostered his determination and strategic acumen.

In 1147, at the age of fourteen, Henry made his first attempt to secure the English throne, although it was ultimately unsuccessful. However, his persistence and military skill began to earn him a reputation as a formidable leader. By 1153, Henry had gained significant support both in England and on the continent. The Treaty of Wallingford, signed that year, recognized him as Stephen's heir, effectively ending the civil war. Stephen's death in 1154 paved the way for Henry to ascend to the throne as Henry II.

Henry's coronation on December 19, 1154, marked the beginning of a reign that would be characterized by extensive administrative reforms and territorial expansion. One of Henry's primary objectives was to restore and strengthen royal authority, which had been significantly weakened during The Anarchy. He set about consolidating his power by curbing the influence of the barons and restoring royal control over the courts and the treasury.

A significant aspect of Henry's legacy was his legal reforms, which laid the groundwork for the English common law system. He introduced the Assize of Clarendon in 1166, which established procedures for criminal justice and initiated the use of juries in legal proceedings. This reform aimed to standardize the administration of justice and reduce the arbitrary power of local lords. The development of common law under Henry II provided a more consistent and equitable legal framework, which has had a lasting impact on the English legal system.

Henry's ambitious nature extended beyond legal reforms; he was also a keen military strategist and sought to expand his dominions. Through his marriage to Eleanor of Aquitaine in 1152, Henry acquired vast territories in France, including Aquitaine, Poitou, and Gascony. This union significantly increased his power and wealth, making him one of the most formidable rulers in Europe. Henry's continental possessions, known as the Angevin Empire, spanned from the Scottish border to the Pyrenees, encompassing large parts of modern-day France and England.

Despite his successes, Henry's reign was marred by conflicts with his own family. His marriage to Eleanor of Aquitaine, though initially advantageous, became increasingly strained over time. Eleanor, a powerful and influential figure in her own right, chafed under Henry's control and supported their sons in their rebellions against him. Henry and Eleanor had eight children, including five sons who played significant roles in the political landscape of the time: William, who died young; Henry the Young King; Richard (later Richard the Lionheart); Geoffrey; and John (later King John).

The most notable and tumultuous of these family conflicts was the rebellion of Henry's sons in 1173-1174, known as the Revolt of 1173-1174. Encouraged by Eleanor, who was subsequently imprisoned by Henry, the rebellion was led by Henry the Young King, Richard, and Geoffrey, with the support of several powerful barons and foreign allies, including King Louis VII of France. Despite the formidable coalition against him, Henry II's military and strategic prowess ultimately prevailed, and the rebellion was quashed. However, the revolt left deep scars within the family and highlighted the ongoing struggle for power and authority within the Angevin Empire.

Another significant conflict during Henry's reign was his dispute with Thomas Becket, the Archbishop of Canterbury. Initially, Henry and Becket were close allies, and Henry appointed Becket as Archbishop in 1162, hoping to assert greater control over the Church. However, Becket's growing independence and opposition to Henry's attempts to reduce clerical privileges led to a bitter and protracted conflict. The dispute centered on the jurisdiction of secular courts over clergy and the authority of the monarchy over the Church.

The conflict reached a tragic climax in 1170 when Becket was murdered by four knights in Canterbury Cathedral, allegedly on Henry's instigation. The murder shocked Christendom and severely damaged Henry's reputation. In an effort to atone for Becket's death and restore his standing with the Church, Henry performed public penance and reconciled with the papacy. Despite this, the Becket affair left a lasting impact on Henry's reign and highlighted the ongoing tensions between the monarchy and the Church.

Throughout his reign, Henry II faced numerous external threats and engaged in several military campaigns to defend and expand his territories. He successfully subdued rebellions in Wales and Ireland, establishing English dominance in these regions. In Ireland, Henry's intervention in 1171-1172 led to the establishment of English rule, beginning a complex and often contentious relationship between the two countries that would persist for centuries.

Henry's relations with Scotland were also significant. In 1174, during the Revolt of 1173-1174, King William the Lion of Scotland invaded northern England but was captured at the Battle of Alnwick. As a result, William was forced to sign the Treaty of Falaise, acknowledging Henry as his overlord and strengthening English influence over Scotland.

Despite his many accomplishments, Henry II's final years were marked by personal and political turmoil. The death of his heir, Henry the Young King, in 1183, led to further conflicts with his surviving sons, Richard and John. The relationship between Henry and Richard, in particular, became increasingly strained. Richard, who had emerged as a formidable military leader in his own right, resented his father's attempts to curtail his power in Aquitaine. By 1188, Richard had allied with King Philip II of France, and the two launched a concerted campaign against Henry.

In 1189, facing defeat and suffering from illness, Henry was forced to negotiate with his rebellious son and the French king. The Treaty of Azay-le-Rideau marked the end of Henry's resistance. Broken and humiliated, Henry II retreated to Chinon, where he died on July 6, 1189. His death marked the end of an era and paved the way for Richard the Lionheart to ascend to the throne.

Henry II's legacy is multifaceted and enduring. His legal reforms laid the foundations for the English common law system, which has had a profound and lasting impact on legal traditions in many parts of the world. His efforts to centralize royal authority and reduce the power of the barons helped to stabilize and strengthen the English monarchy. Henry's territorial ambitions and military campaigns significantly shaped the political landscape of medieval Europe and established the foundations of the Angevin Empire.

Despite his achievements, Henry's reign was also marked by significant challenges and conflicts. His turbulent relationships with his family, particularly his wife Eleanor and his sons, underscored the difficulties of maintaining control over a vast and diverse empire. The Becket affair and the resulting tensions with the Church highlighted the complex and often fraught relationship between secular and ecclesiastical authority.

In the centuries since his death, Henry II has been remembered as a complex and dynamic figure, a ruler of considerable vision and ambition whose reign left an indelible mark on English and European history. His life and legacy continue to be the subject of historical study and debate, reflecting the enduring fascination with one of the most significant monarchs of the medieval period.

Chapter 29: Queen Isabella I of Castile

Queen Isabella I of Castile, born on April 22, 1451, in Madrigal de las Altas Torres, was a formidable and pivotal figure in Spanish and European history. Her reign from 1474 until her death in 1504 was marked by significant political, military, and religious changes that laid the groundwork for the modern Spanish state. Her legacy includes the unification of Spain, the completion of the Reconquista, the sponsorship of Christopher Columbus's 1492 voyage, and the establishment of the Spanish Inquisition.

Isabella was the daughter of John II of Castile and his second wife, Isabella of Portugal. Her early years were spent in relative obscurity, as she was not initially in line for the throne. However, the death of her half-brother, King Henry IV of Castile's only legitimate son, Alfonso, in 1468, and the subsequent political turmoil, thrust her into the center of the Castilian succession crisis. Her half-brother, Henry IV, recognized her as his heir over his daughter Joanna, a decision that set the stage for her future rule.

Isabella's path to the throne was fraught with challenges and political maneuvering. The Castilian nobility was deeply divided, with factions supporting either Isabella or Joanna, nicknamed "La Beltraneja" due to doubts about her paternity. In 1469, Isabella made a politically astute marriage to Ferdinand of Aragon, a union that would later bring about the unification of Spain. Their marriage was initially opposed by Henry IV and various noble factions, but Isabella's determination and political skill prevailed.

Upon Henry IV's death in 1474, Isabella swiftly claimed the throne of Castile, sparking a five-year war of succession against the supporters of Joanna, who was backed by Portugal. The war concluded in 1479 with the Treaty of Alcáçovas, which recognized Isabella as the undisputed queen of Castile. This victory solidified her position and allowed her to begin the process of consolidating her power and implementing her vision for a unified Spain.

Isabella's reign, in conjunction with Ferdinand, marked a period of significant political and administrative reforms. The couple worked tirelessly to strengthen royal authority, reduce the power of the nobility, and restore law and order throughout Castile. One of their most notable achievements was the establishment of the Santa Hermandad, a national police force aimed at curbing the lawlessness and banditry that plagued the kingdom. This force played a crucial role in restoring peace and stability.

The unification of Castile and Aragon through Isabella and Ferdinand's marriage was a monumental step toward the creation of a single Spanish state. Although the two kingdoms retained separate institutions, laws, and customs, the monarchs ruled jointly and pursued a common policy. Their combined efforts in both domestic and foreign affairs significantly enhanced their power and influence.

One of the most enduring legacies of Isabella's reign was the completion of the Reconquista, the centuries-long effort to reclaim the Iberian Peninsula from Muslim rule. The final chapter of the Reconquista culminated in the conquest of Granada in 1492, the last Muslim stronghold in Spain. The fall of Granada was not only a military triumph but also a symbol of religious and cultural unification under Christian rule. This victory allowed Isabella and Ferdinand to consolidate their authority and embark on a period of religious and cultural transformation.

A critical aspect of this transformation was the establishment of the Spanish Inquisition in 1478. The Inquisition, authorized by Pope Sixtus IV but driven by the Spanish monarchs, aimed to maintain Catholic orthodoxy and root out heresy within their realms. While it initially targeted converted Jews and Muslims suspected of secretly practicing their former faiths, its scope eventually widened to include a broad range of perceived heresies. The Inquisition's methods were often brutal, involving torture and public executions, and it became a powerful tool for maintaining religious and political control.

The Inquisition also led to the expulsion of the Jews from Spain in 1492, an edict that had profound economic and cultural consequences. The decision to expel the Jewish population, who were given the choice of conversion or exile, was motivated by a combination of religious zeal and political pragmatism. The departure of many skilled and educated individuals had a lasting impact on Spanish society, economy, and culture.

Isabella's reign was also marked by her patronage of exploration and her support for Christopher Columbus's 1492 voyage across the Atlantic. Columbus's expedition, sponsored by Isabella, resulted in the European discovery of the Americas, opening up new territories for Spanish conquest and colonization. This monumental event marked the beginning of the Spanish Empire and initiated a period of exploration, conquest, and exploitation that would have profound implications for both the Old and New Worlds.

The wealth and resources acquired from the New World significantly enhanced Spain's power and influence, setting the stage for its emergence as a dominant global empire. Isabella's support for Columbus and other explorers demonstrated her vision and ambition, as well as her ability to recognize and seize opportunities for expanding her realm.

Isabella's personal life was deeply intertwined with her political ambitions. She and Ferdinand had five surviving children: Isabella, John, Joanna, Maria, and Catherine. Their marriages were carefully arranged to strengthen alliances and consolidate power. Isabella's daughter Joanna, known as Joanna the Mad, would eventually inherit both Castile and Aragon, although her reign was marred by her mental instability and the political machinations of her father and later her son, Charles V.

Catherine of Aragon's marriage to Henry VIII of England would have significant implications for both English and Spanish history. Catherine's failure to produce a male heir led to Henry VIII's divorce and the subsequent break with the Roman Catholic Church, initiating the English Reformation. Thus, Isabella's dynastic ambitions and the marriages of her children had far-reaching consequences that extended well beyond her own reign.

Isabella was not only a political and military leader but also a devout Catholic who saw her role as a defender of the faith. Her personal piety influenced many of her policies, including her support for the Inquisition and the expulsion of the Jews. She was also a patron of education and culture, founding institutions such as the University of Alcalá and supporting the arts and scholarship. Her court became a center of learning and culture, attracting scholars, artists, and theologians.

Isabella's health began to decline in the early 1500s, and she made arrangements for the succession to ensure the stability of her realms. She died on November 26, 1504, in Medina del Campo. Her death marked the end of an era, but her legacy endured through the institutions she helped build and the policies she implemented.

Chapter 30: Emperor Suleiman of Ottoman Empire

Emperor Suleiman the Magnificent, also known as Suleiman I, was born on November 6, 1494, in Trabzon, a port city on the Black Sea coast. He was the tenth and longest-reigning Sultan of the Ottoman Empire, ruling from 1520 until his death in 1566. Suleiman's reign is often regarded as the apex of Ottoman power, cultural achievement, and administrative sophistication. His influence extended across vast territories in Europe, Asia, and Africa, making the Ottoman Empire one of the most formidable political entities of the 16th century.

Suleiman ascended to the throne at the age of 26, following the death of his father, Sultan Selim I, in 1520. His early education was overseen by renowned scholars and statesmen, ensuring he was well-versed in the art of governance, military strategy, and Islamic jurisprudence. Suleiman's formative years were spent in the provincial capitals of Manisa and Istanbul, where he honed his skills in leadership and administration.

Suleiman's reign began with a series of military campaigns aimed at consolidating and expanding Ottoman territories. One of his first major undertakings was the siege of Belgrade in 1521. Belgrade was a strategic fortress on the Danube River, crucial for the control of southeastern Europe. The successful capture of Belgrade not only bolstered Ottoman control in the Balkans but also set the stage for further expansion into Europe.

In 1522, Suleiman turned his attention to the island of Rhodes, a stronghold of the Knights Hospitaller. The siege of Rhodes was a significant military endeavor, marked by intense combat and strategic maneuvers. After a protracted and grueling siege, the island capitulated, and the Knights were allowed to leave under honorable terms. The capture of Rhodes secured Ottoman dominance in the eastern

Mediterranean and showcased Suleiman's commitment to extending his empire's reach.

One of the most defining moments of Suleiman's military career was the Battle of Mohács in 1526. Facing the Kingdom of Hungary, Suleiman led his forces to a decisive victory, effectively crippling Hungarian power and paving the way for Ottoman influence in Central Europe. The aftermath of Mohács saw the establishment of Ottoman suzerainty over Hungary, though it also led to decades of conflict as European powers, particularly the Habsburgs, resisted Ottoman expansion.

The siege of Vienna in 1529 marked another ambitious campaign by Suleiman. Although the siege ultimately failed, it demonstrated the extent of Ottoman military prowess and struck fear into the heart of Europe. The failure to capture Vienna did not deter Suleiman from continuing his efforts to expand Ottoman influence in Europe, and subsequent campaigns maintained pressure on the Habsburg territories.

Suleiman's reign was not solely defined by his military conquests. He was also a patron of the arts, architecture, and education, earning him the title "the Magnificent" in the West and "Kanuni" (the Lawgiver) in the East. His legal reforms were particularly noteworthy, as he sought to harmonize the various legal traditions within his empire and create a cohesive legal system. The Kanun, a set of administrative and fiscal laws, complemented the Sharia (Islamic law) and provided a framework for governance that was both efficient and just.

Suleiman's interest in architecture and the arts led to a flourishing of Ottoman culture. The most prominent architect of his time, Mimar Sinan, was responsible for designing some of the most iconic structures in the Ottoman Empire. The Suleymaniye Mosque in Istanbul, built in honor of Suleiman, remains a masterpiece of Islamic architecture. Its grandeur and architectural innovation reflect the zenith of Ottoman artistic achievement during Suleiman's reign.

The imperial court under Suleiman was a vibrant center of cultural and intellectual activity. Poets, scholars, and artists were patronized, contributing to a rich cultural milieu. Suleiman himself was an accomplished poet, writing under the pen name "Muhibbi." His poetry, along with that of his contemporaries, formed an essential part of the Ottoman literary tradition.

Suleiman's domestic policies were aimed at strengthening the central authority and improving the welfare of his subjects. He undertook significant administrative reforms to streamline the bureaucracy and enhance the efficiency of governance. His reign saw the construction of roads, bridges, and public buildings, which facilitated trade and communication across the vast empire. The improvements in infrastructure not only bolstered the economy but also helped to integrate the diverse regions of the empire more closely.

One of the most enduring aspects of Suleiman's legacy was his relationship with his chief consort and later wife, Hurrem Sultan, also known as Roxelana. Hurrem was a former slave who rose to become Suleiman's most trusted advisor and the mother of several of his children. Her influence in the court and over Suleiman himself was unprecedented, challenging traditional norms and reshaping the dynamics of the Ottoman harem. Hurrem's involvement in political and diplomatic affairs marked a significant departure from the conventional roles of women in the empire and left a lasting impact on Ottoman history.

The latter part of Suleiman's reign was marked by continued military campaigns, as well as growing internal challenges. The long-standing conflict with the Safavid Empire in Persia persisted, with both sides vying for control over the contested territories of Mesopotamia and the Caucasus. These conflicts drained resources and required sustained military effort, yet they also underscored the strategic importance of these regions to both empires.

Suleiman's death on September 6, 1566, during the siege of Szigetvár in Hungary, marked the end of an era. His death was kept secret for a time to ensure the stability of the Ottoman forces and the smooth succession of his son, Selim II. Suleiman's legacy as a military leader, lawgiver, and patron of the arts and culture left an indelible mark on the Ottoman Empire and the broader Islamic world.

In assessing Suleiman's impact, it is essential to consider both his achievements and the broader context of his reign. His military campaigns significantly expanded the Ottoman Empire's territory and influence, establishing it as a dominant power in Europe, Asia, and Africa. His legal and administrative reforms brought greater cohesion and efficiency to the governance of the empire, while his patronage of the arts and architecture enriched Ottoman cultural life.

However, Suleiman's reign also faced significant challenges and complexities. The constant military campaigns placed a heavy burden on the empire's resources and often led to protracted conflicts with powerful adversaries. The internal dynamics of the court, particularly the influence of Hurrem Sultan and the succession struggles among Suleiman's sons, revealed the intricacies and potential vulnerabilities of Ottoman political life.

Suleiman's efforts to balance the demands of military expansion, legal reform, and cultural patronage highlight the multifaceted nature of his rule. His ability to maintain stability and foster growth in such a vast and diverse empire speaks to his skill as a ruler and his vision for the future of the Ottoman state.

Suleiman's legacy continues to resonate in contemporary discussions of Ottoman history and its place in the broader context of world history. His reign represents a period of unparalleled achievement and transformation, shaping the course of the Ottoman Empire and leaving a lasting imprint on the regions it encompassed. As both a historical figure and a symbol of imperial grandeur, Suleiman the Magnificent remains a central figure in the study of the Ottoman Empire and its enduring legacy.

Chapter 31: King Henry VIII of England

King Henry VIII of England, born on June 28, 1491, at Greenwich Palace, was the second son of King Henry VII and Elizabeth of York. His reign from 1509 to 1547 is one of the most dramatic and consequential periods in English history. Henry VIII is best known for his six marriages, his role in the separation of the Church of England from the Roman Catholic Church, and his significant impact on the English monarchy and state. His reign marked the beginning of the English Reformation and laid the groundwork for the modern British state.

Henry VIII's early life was marked by an education befitting a prince of the Renaissance. Fluent in Latin and French, and skilled in theology and philosophy, he was also athletic, enjoying hunting, jousting, and tennis. Henry was not initially destined for the throne; his older brother Arthur was the heir. However, Arthur's death in 1502 left Henry as the next in line. Upon his father's death in 1509, Henry ascended the throne at the age of 17 and married his brother's widow, Catherine of Aragon, shortly thereafter. This marriage was initially supported by a papal dispensation due to the biblical prohibition against marrying a brother's widow.

Henry's early reign was characterized by his military ambitions and desire to assert England's power in Europe. His initial campaigns against France were motivated by a desire to reclaim English territories and establish himself as a formidable European monarch. The Battle of the Spurs in 1513 and the subsequent capture of the French town of Tournai were significant, although these gains were short-lived. Henry's alliances and conflicts with France and the Holy Roman Empire were part of the larger struggle for dominance in Renaissance Europe.

One of the most enduring aspects of Henry's legacy is his tumultuous marital history, driven largely by his desire for a male heir to secure the Tudor dynasty. His marriage to Catherine of Aragon produced only one surviving child, Mary, and no male heirs. This failure led Henry to seek an annulment of his marriage to Catherine, which the Pope refused to grant. Henry's determination to secure a divorce led to the English Reformation, a seismic shift in English religious and political life.

In 1533, Henry married Anne Boleyn, a move that precipitated the break with Rome. The Archbishop of Canterbury, Thomas Cranmer, declared Henry's marriage to Catherine null and void and validated his marriage to Anne. This act was followed by the passage of the Act of Supremacy in 1534, which declared Henry the Supreme Head of the Church of England. This severed ties with the Catholic Church and placed the king at the head of the new Anglican Church. The dissolution of the monasteries between 1536 and 1541 further consolidated Henry's control over the church's wealth and land.

Anne Boleyn's failure to produce a male heir, giving birth instead to Elizabeth, led to her downfall. Accused of adultery, treason, and incest, she was executed in 1536. Henry quickly remarried Jane Seymour, who gave birth to his only male heir, Edward, in 1537 but died shortly after childbirth. Henry's subsequent marriages to Anne of Cleves, Catherine Howard, and Catherine Parr were marked by political maneuvering, personal intrigue, and further executions. Anne of Cleves, whom Henry married in 1540, was divorced after six months; Catherine Howard was executed for adultery in 1542; and Catherine Parr outlived Henry, dying in 1548.

Henry's reign also saw significant changes in the structure and administration of the English government. He centralized power, reducing the influence of the nobility and increasing the authority of the monarchy. This was achieved through the establishment of a more professional bureaucracy and the expansion of royal prerogatives. The legal reforms enacted during his reign laid the foundations for a modern state, enhancing the efficiency and reach of royal administration.

The Henrician Reformation had profound implications for religious life in England. The dissolution of the monasteries not only transferred vast amounts of wealth and land to the Crown and loyal subjects but also led to significant social and economic disruption. The suppression of Catholic institutions and the establishment of the Anglican Church under royal control reshaped religious practice and belief, although the extent of doctrinal change was initially limited.

Henry's policies towards Ireland and Scotland were marked by attempts to extend and consolidate English control. His reign saw the Tudor conquest of Ireland begin in earnest, with efforts to impose English law and governance. In Scotland, his ambitions were thwarted by resistance and the traditional enmity between the two nations. The marriage of his sister Margaret to James IV of Scotland, however, would eventually lead to the Union of the Crowns under their great-grandson, James VI and I.

Henry's later years were marked by increasing authoritarianism, health problems, and financial strain. His extravagant lifestyle and continuous military campaigns, particularly against France and Scotland, drained the royal coffers. The imposition of heavy taxes and the debasement of the coinage led to economic difficulties and popular discontent. Henry's physical decline, exacerbated by obesity and possible untreated diabetes, affected his ability to govern effectively in his final years.

Despite these challenges, Henry VIII's reign left an indelible mark on English history. The establishment of the Church of England and the assertion of royal supremacy had lasting religious and political implications. His efforts to strengthen the monarchy and centralize administrative control laid the groundwork for the future development of the British state. The cultural and intellectual achievements of the

Henrician court, often overshadowed by his marital and political dramas, also contributed to the Renaissance in England.

Henry's legacy is a complex one, encompassing both his achievements and his failures. His determination to secure a male heir and establish a stable dynasty drove much of his policy and personal life, often with dramatic and bloody consequences. His reign saw significant changes in the relationship between the Crown and its subjects, the church and the state, and England's position in the broader European context.

Chapter 32: Queen Catherine de' Medici of France

Queen Catherine de' Medici, born on April 13, 1519, in Florence, Italy, was one of the most influential figures of the French Renaissance and played a pivotal role in the complex political and religious dynamics of 16th-century France. As the wife of King Henry II and the mother of three French kings, Catherine's influence extended far beyond her role as queen consort. Her life was marked by political intrigue, religious conflict, and her efforts to maintain the stability of the French monarchy during one of its most turbulent periods.

Catherine was born into the powerful Medici family, which had established itself as a leading political and banking dynasty in Florence. Her father, Lorenzo II de' Medici, was the Duke of Urbino, and her mother, Madeleine de La Tour d'Auvergne, was a French noblewoman. Orphaned at a young age, Catherine was raised by various relatives and placed in convents for her education. Despite her challenging early life, she received a comprehensive education that prepared her for the complexities of court life and governance.

In 1533, at the age of 14, Catherine married Henry, Duke of Orleans, the second son of King Francis I of France. This marriage was part of a strategic alliance between France and the Medici family, aimed at strengthening their political and economic ties. Initially, Catherine's position at the French court was relatively weak, overshadowed by her husband's mistress, Diane de Poitiers, and the lack of immediate heirs. However, Catherine's fortunes changed when Henry became king in 1547, making her queen consort.

As queen, Catherine faced significant challenges, particularly in producing male heirs to secure the Valois dynasty. Her first ten years of marriage were marked by a lack of pregnancies, causing concern about the future of the royal lineage. However, she eventually gave birth to ten children, of whom seven survived infancies. Her sons Francis II, Charles IX, and Henry III would each become kings of France, while her daughters made strategic marriages into other European royal families.

Catherine's political influence grew significantly after the death of her husband, Henry II, in 1559. Henry's death was sudden and tragic, resulting from a jousting accident during a tournament held to celebrate the marriage of their daughter, Elizabeth, to Philip II of Spain. With the ascension of her eldest son, Francis II, to the throne, Catherine assumed the role of regent, given Francis's youth and inexperience. Her regency was marked by her efforts to navigate the treacherous waters of French politics, characterized by factionalism and religious strife.

One of the most pressing issues during Catherine's regency and throughout her life was the conflict between Catholics and Huguenots (French Protestants). The Reformation had spread across Europe, and France was no exception, with Protestantism gaining a significant following. This religious divide led to a series of wars known as the French Wars of Religion, which would plague France for decades. Catherine's primary goal was to maintain the stability and unity of the French state, often through a policy of political and religious compromise.

Catherine's approach to religious conflict was pragmatic and sometimes ruthless. She sought to balance the power of the Catholic Guise family and the Protestant Bourbon faction, often employing marriage alliances and shifting political alliances to maintain equilibrium. One of her most controversial actions was her involvement in the St. Bartholomew's Day Massacre in 1572. This event, which began as a targeted assassination of Huguenot leaders in Paris and escalated into widespread slaughter, has been a subject of intense historical debate. Some historians argue that Catherine played a central role in orchestrating the massacre, while others contend that she was trying to prevent further escalation of violence and maintain royal authority.

Catherine's role as a mother was deeply intertwined with her political maneuvering. She sought to secure advantageous marriages for her children to strengthen France's alliances and consolidate her own power. Her daughter, Marguerite de Valois, was married to Henry of Navarre (later Henry IV of France), a union intended to bridge the divide between Catholics and Protestants. This marriage, however, was fraught with tension and conflict, reflecting the broader religious turmoil of the period.

The reigns of Catherine's sons were marked by instability and conflict, with Catherine often serving as the de facto ruler and advisor. Francis II's brief reign was dominated by the influence of the powerful Guise family. After Francis's death in 1560, Charles IX ascended to the throne, and Catherine continued to play a central role as regent. Charles's reign was plagued by the ongoing wars of religion, and Catherine's efforts to broker peace were frequently undermined by the deep-seated animosities between Catholics and Protestants.

The ascension of Henry III in 1574 brought new challenges. Henry's reign was marked by internal strife and declining royal authority. Catherine's influence waned as Henry sought to assert his own control, but she remained a key figure in the court, advising her son and attempting to mediate between rival factions. Henry III's assassination in 1589 marked the end of the Valois dynasty, and Catherine did not live to see the resolution of the religious conflicts that had defined her life.

Catherine de' Medici's legacy is complex and multifaceted. She has been both vilified and praised by historians, often depicted as a Machiavellian figure who wielded power through manipulation and intrigue. Her efforts to maintain the Valois dynasty and stabilize France during a period of profound religious and political upheaval required a delicate balance of diplomacy, pragmatism, and, at times, ruthless action.

Catherine's cultural patronage also left a lasting impact on France. She was a patron of the arts, supporting artists, architects, and musicians. Her influence extended to the development of the French Renaissance, and she played a key role in introducing Italian cultural practices to France. The construction of the Tuileries Palace and the expansion of the Louvre were among her notable contributions to French architecture.

Chapter 33: Queen Mary I of England

Queen Mary I of England, also known as Mary Tudor and famously remembered as "Bloody Mary," was born on February 18, 1516, at the Palace of Placentia in Greenwich, England. She was the only surviving child of King Henry VIII and his first wife, Catherine of Aragon. Mary's life and reign were marked by religious turmoil, political strife, and her fervent attempts to restore Roman Catholicism in England after her father's break with the Catholic Church.

Mary's early life was one of privilege but also of political significance. As the daughter of the king, she was given a comprehensive education, learning Latin, Spanish, French, and some Italian, as well as studying music, dance, and theology. Her early childhood was relatively stable, but her life took a dramatic turn when her father sought to annul his marriage to her mother in order to marry Anne Boleyn. The subsequent fallout from Henry VIII's efforts to secure a male heir and his separation from the Catholic Church profoundly impacted Mary's life.

When Henry VIII declared his marriage to Catherine null and void in 1533 and married Anne Boleyn, Mary was declared illegitimate and stripped of her title of princess. She was forced to live as Lady Mary, away from her mother, and her household was drastically reduced. Despite these humiliations, Mary remained devoted to her Catholic faith and her mother. Catherine's death in 1536 was a significant blow to Mary, but she continued to resist the pressure to conform to her father's new religious policies.

The death of Anne Boleyn and the subsequent marriages of Henry VIII did little to improve Mary's situation. It was not until Henry's marriage to Jane Seymour, who sympathized with Mary and worked to reconcile her with her father, that Mary's status improved somewhat. Mary was finally restored to the line of succession in 1544, behind her half-brother Edward and her half-sister Elizabeth, through the Act of Succession.

Upon Henry VIII's death in 1547, his son Edward VI ascended the throne. Edward's reign further entrenched Protestant reforms, which were anathema to Mary. During this period, Mary lived quietly but firmly resisted any attempt to make her renounce her Catholic faith. Edward VI's health began to decline rapidly in 1553, leading to a crisis of succession. The Protestant faction, led by John Dudley, Duke of Northumberland, sought to prevent Mary from becoming queen by naming Lady Jane Grey, a Protestant and great-granddaughter of Henry VII, as Edward's successor.

Mary, however, garnered significant popular support. When Edward VI died on July 6, 1553, Mary swiftly moved to assert her claim to the throne. She fled to East Anglia, where she gathered supporters and raised an army. The popular and military support for Mary quickly overwhelmed Dudley's plans, and Mary triumphantly entered London on August 3, 1553, to claim her throne. Lady Jane Grey's reign lasted a mere nine days, and she was subsequently imprisoned and later executed.

Mary's ascension to the throne was met with widespread jubilation, as many Englishmen were hopeful that the return of a Tudor monarch would bring stability. However, Mary's reign soon became one of the most contentious and turbulent periods in English history. Her primary goal was to restore Roman Catholicism as the state religion, reversing the Protestant reforms enacted during her father's and brother's reigns. This goal put her on a collision course with the Protestant establishment and a significant portion of her subjects.

One of Mary's first acts as queen was to repeal the religious laws enacted during Edward VI's reign, effectively undoing the Protestant reforms. She restored the Latin Mass and the traditional Catholic practices. These actions were bolstered by the return of Cardinal Reginald Pole, a staunch Catholic, as the papal legate and later

Archbishop of Canterbury. Pole played a crucial role in guiding Mary's religious policies and in the reestablishment of the Catholic hierarchy in England.

Mary's marriage to Philip II of Spain in 1554 was a key component of her strategy to restore Catholicism and strengthen England's ties with Catholic Europe. The marriage treaty was carefully negotiated to ensure that Philip would not gain any sovereign authority over England and that England would not be drawn into Spanish wars. However, the marriage was deeply unpopular among her subjects, who feared Spanish domination and resented Philip's foreign influence.

The union with Philip II failed to produce the desired heir, with Mary experiencing false pregnancies that deepened her personal and political despair. The lack of an heir also meant that the Protestant Elizabeth remained the likely successor, a prospect that troubled Mary deeply.

Mary's most infamous legacy stems from her persecution of Protestants, which earned her the moniker "Bloody Mary." In an effort to enforce religious conformity, Mary and her government conducted a campaign of persecution against Protestant dissenters. Between 1555 and 1558, approximately 280 Protestants were burned at the stake for heresy, including notable figures such as bishops Hugh Latimer, Nicholas Ridley, and Thomas Cranmer, the former Archbishop of Canterbury. These executions were part of a broader campaign to root out Protestantism and restore Catholic orthodoxy.

The Marian persecutions had the opposite effect of what Mary intended. Instead of quelling Protestant dissent, they generated widespread sympathy for the martyrs and solidified opposition to her reign. The brutal nature of the executions and the steadfastness of the victims in the face of death were vividly recorded in works such as John Foxe's "Book of Martyrs," which portrayed them as heroic defenders of the true faith against tyrannical oppression.

Mary's foreign policy was also marked by difficulties. Her marriage to Philip II dragged England into the Habsburg-Valois conflict, culminating in the loss of Calais, England's last possession on the continent, to France in 1558. The loss of Calais was a significant blow to national pride and Mary's prestige.

Mary's health began to decline in 1558, and it became clear that she would not produce an heir. On November 17, 1558, Mary died at St. James's Palace in London, likely from uterine or ovarian cancer. Her death marked the end of an era and the beginning of the Elizabethan Age, as her half-sister Elizabeth ascended the throne.

Queen Mary I's reign is often viewed through the lens of her failed attempts to restore Catholicism and the brutal methods she employed to achieve that goal. However, her reign also highlighted the deep religious divisions within England and the complexities of navigating political and religious change. Despite her sincere efforts to return her kingdom to what she believed was the true faith, Mary's actions ultimately strengthened the Protestant cause and set the stage for the religious settlement of her successor, Elizabeth I.

In retrospect, Mary's reign is a poignant reminder of the perils and challenges of religious reform and the intense personal and political struggles that characterized the Tudor period. Her life and legacy are marked by her unwavering faith, her determination to restore her mother's honor and religious heritage, and the profound impact she had on English history, both during her life and in the centuries that followed.

Chapter 34: Queen Elizabeth I of England

Queen Elizabeth I of England, often referred to as the "Virgin Queen," ruled England from 1558 until her death in 1603, a period known as the Elizabethan Era. Born on September 7, 1533, at Greenwich Palace to King Henry VIII and his second wife, Anne Boleyn, Elizabeth's early life was fraught with political intrigue, religious turmoil, and personal danger. Her reign, however, became one of the most celebrated periods in English history, marked by the flourishing of English drama, the defeat of the Spanish Armada, and the establishment of a Protestant church that shaped the future of England.

Elizabeth's birth was initially a disappointment to her father, Henry VIII, who had desperately sought a male heir to secure the Tudor dynasty. Anne Boleyn's inability to provide a male successor led to her downfall and execution in 1536 when Elizabeth was just two and a half years old. Declared illegitimate and stripped of her title of princess, Elizabeth faced an uncertain future. Despite this, she received a rigorous education under the tutelage of scholars like Roger Ascham, mastering Latin, Greek, French, and Italian, as well as studying philosophy, history, and rhetoric. This education equipped her with the intellectual tools she would later use to navigate the treacherous political landscape of England.

Following Henry VIII's death in 1547, Elizabeth's half-brother Edward VI ascended to the throne. During Edward's reign, Elizabeth's life was relatively stable, though she remained vigilant against political machinations. Upon Edward's death in 1553, the throne passed briefly to Lady Jane Grey before being claimed by Elizabeth's half-sister, Mary I. Mary's reign was marked by her efforts to restore Roman Catholicism and her marriage to Philip II of Spain, which faced significant opposition from the English public. Elizabeth, a Protestant and seen as a legitimate heir by many, was imprisoned in the Tower of London under suspicion of supporting Protestant rebellions. However, her cautious and intelligent conduct during this period helped her survive and eventually ascend the throne.

Elizabeth became queen on November 17, 1558, following Mary's death. Her accession was met with widespread relief and enthusiasm from a populace weary of religious strife and foreign influence. One of Elizabeth's first acts as queen was to establish a religious settlement that would restore Protestantism while seeking to unify the country. The Elizabethan Religious Settlement, encapsulated in the Act of Supremacy (1559) and the Act of Uniformity (1559), re-established the Church of England's independence from Rome and set out a moderate Protestant doctrine that aimed to accommodate as many subjects as possible. This settlement established Elizabeth as the Supreme Governor of the Church of England and required adherence to the Book of Common Prayer.

Elizabeth's reign was characterized by cautious but effective governance. She surrounded herself with capable advisors, most notably William Cecil, Lord Burghley, who served as her chief advisor for most of her reign. Her government was adept at balancing the various factions within her court and managing relations with other European powers. Elizabeth's foreign policy was pragmatic and aimed at maintaining England's independence while avoiding costly wars. She skillfully played the major Catholic powers, Spain and France, against each other, often using marriage negotiations as a diplomatic tool, though she never married herself.

One of the most significant challenges of Elizabeth's reign was the threat posed by Mary, Queen of Scots. Mary, a Catholic and Elizabeth's cousin, was seen by many Catholics as the legitimate ruler of England. After being deposed in Scotland, Mary sought refuge in England in 1568, where she became the focus of Catholic plots to overthrow Elizabeth. These plots, such as the Ridolfi Plot (1571) and the

Babington Plot (1586), aimed to assassinate Elizabeth and place Mary on the throne. Elizabeth's government, with the help of her spymaster Sir Francis Walsingham, uncovered these conspiracies, leading to Mary's imprisonment and eventual execution in 1587.

Elizabeth's reign also saw the rise of English seafaring and exploration. Figures like Sir Francis Drake and Sir Walter Raleigh expanded English influence overseas and challenged Spanish dominance. Drake's circumnavigation of the globe (1577–1580) and his raids on Spanish treasure fleets showcased English naval prowess. The most significant maritime conflict of Elizabeth's reign was the defeat of the Spanish Armada in 1588. Philip II of Spain, seeking to invade England and restore Catholicism, sent a massive fleet to England. However, the English navy, aided by favorable weather conditions, managed to repel the Armada. This victory bolstered Elizabeth's popularity and established England as a formidable naval power.

Culturally, the Elizabethan Era was a golden age for English literature and the arts. The period saw the flourishing of English drama, with playwrights such as William Shakespeare, Christopher Marlowe, and Ben Jonson producing works that have become central to the Western literary canon. The patronage of the arts by Elizabeth and her courtiers helped create an environment in which creativity could thrive. The era also witnessed advancements in poetry, music, and architecture, contributing to the cultural legacy that defines the period.

Elizabeth's personal life and image were central to her reign. Known for her intelligence, wit, and charismatic presence, she cultivated an image of the "Virgin Queen," dedicated solely to her country. This image was reinforced by her elaborate court rituals, her portraits, and her speeches, such as the famous Tilbury speech delivered to her troops as they prepared to defend against the Spanish Armada. Her decision not to marry, despite numerous suitors and diplomatic marriage proposals, allowed her to maintain control over her kingdom and avoid the complications of foreign alliances.

Despite her successes, Elizabeth's reign was not without challenges and criticisms. Economic difficulties, including inflation and poor harvests, led to social unrest and hardship for many of her subjects. The later years of her reign saw increased taxation and discontent, culminating in the Essex Rebellion of 1601, led by Robert Devereux, Earl of Essex, a former favorite of the queen. The rebellion was quickly suppressed, and Essex was executed, but it underscored the tensions and challenges of Elizabeth's later years.

Elizabeth's health began to decline in the early 1600s, and the question of succession became increasingly pressing. Having no children, Elizabeth's death on March 24, 1603, marked the end of the Tudor dynasty. She was succeeded by James VI of Scotland, the son of Mary, Queen of Scots, who became James I of England, thus uniting the crowns of England and Scotland. Elizabeth's death was met with mourning and reflection on a reign that had seen England emerge as a significant European power with a vibrant cultural life.

Queen Elizabeth I's legacy is immense and multifaceted. She successfully navigated the treacherous political landscape of her time, established a stable religious settlement, and fostered an environment in which the arts and exploration could flourish. Her reign is often seen as a high point in English history, characterized by relative internal peace, military victories, and cultural achievements. Elizabeth's image as the "Virgin Queen" and her careful management of her public persona have left an enduring mark on English history and popular imagination, cementing her place as one of the most iconic and influential monarchs in English history.

Chapter 35: Emperor Akbar the Great of India

Emperor Akbar the Great, born on October 15, 1542, in Umarkot, Sindh, was one of the most illustrious rulers of the Mughal Empire in India. He ascended the throne in 1556 at the tender age of 13, following the untimely death of his father, Humayun. Akbar's reign, which lasted until his death in 1605, was marked by significant military conquests, administrative innovations, and a policy of religious tolerance that helped to unify a diverse and fragmented Indian subcontinent.

Akbar's early years were spent in a turbulent environment. His father, Humayun, was exiled and struggled to reclaim the Mughal throne from the Afghan leader Sher Shah Suri. During these years of instability, Akbar was raised under the guardianship of his uncle, Askari, in the rugged terrain of the Sindh and Punjab regions. His formative years were shaped by the military campaigns and the nomadic lifestyle of his early life, which later influenced his approach to governance and military strategy.

When Humayun eventually recaptured Delhi in 1555, his reign was short-lived, as he died the following year. This sudden death left the young Akbar in a precarious position. Bairam Khan, a loyal and experienced general, became the regent and protector of the young emperor. Bairam Khan played a crucial role in consolidating Akbar's early rule, notably securing a decisive victory at the Second Battle of Panipat in 1556 against the forces of Hemu, a Hindu king who had declared himself ruler of northern India.

With the threat to his throne neutralized, Akbar began to assert his authority and gradually took control of the administration. By 1560, he dismissed Bairam Khan and assumed full control of the empire. Akbar's reign was characterized by a series of military campaigns that expanded the Mughal Empire's boundaries considerably. He deployed a combination of diplomacy, marriage alliances, and military might to bring various Rajput kingdoms under Mughal suzerainty. The annexation of Rajput territories like Mewar and the strategic matrimonial alliances with Rajput princesses were pivotal in securing the loyalty of these powerful Hindu warriors.

One of Akbar's most notable military achievements was the conquest of Gujarat in 1573. This victory not only expanded the empire but also secured crucial trade routes and ports, boosting the empire's economy. Similarly, his campaigns in Bengal, Bihar, and Orissa extended Mughal influence over eastern India. The incorporation of these diverse regions into the Mughal administrative framework helped to create a more cohesive and unified empire.

Beyond his military conquests, Akbar's administrative reforms were groundbreaking. He established a centralized system of governance that balanced the need for control with local autonomy. Akbar's administration was divided into provinces called Subahs, each governed by a Subahdar. These governors were responsible for maintaining law and order, collecting revenue, and overseeing local administration. The empire was further divided into districts and villages, with officials at each level accountable to higher authorities.

One of Akbar's most significant administrative innovations was the introduction of the Mansabdari system. This system classified officials and military commanders into different ranks or mansabs, based on their service and loyalty to the emperor. Each mansabdar was required to maintain a specified number of cavalrymen, ensuring a ready and reliable military force. The Mansabdari system helped to streamline the administrative hierarchy and ensured that the emperor had direct control over his military and civil officers.

Akbar also implemented a fair and efficient revenue system, designed by his finance minister, Raja Todar Mal. This system, known as the Todar Mal Bandobast or Zabti system, involved detailed surveys and measurements of agricultural land to determine the tax liability of farmers. The tax was fixed at one-third of the produce and could be paid in cash or kind. This reform not only increased state revenue but also reduced the burden on peasants by standardizing tax collection.

One of the most remarkable aspects of Akbar's reign was his policy of religious tolerance and his efforts to foster a syncretic culture. In an era marked by religious conflict, Akbar's inclusive approach was revolutionary. He abolished the jizya, a tax levied on non-Muslims, and allowed freedom of worship for all his subjects. Akbar's court was a melting pot of different cultures and religions, with Hindus, Muslims, Christians, Jains, and Zoroastrians holding important positions.

Akbar's interest in religious and philosophical discussions led to the establishment of the Ibadat Khana (House of Worship) at Fatehpur Sikri, his new capital. Here, he hosted debates and discussions with scholars and theologians of various faiths. These interactions influenced Akbar's own beliefs and culminated in the creation of a new syncretic religion called Din-i-Ilahi, or the "Religion of God." While Din-i-Ilahi did not gain widespread acceptance, it symbolized Akbar's vision of a unified and harmonious empire.

Akbar's patronage of the arts, culture, and architecture also left a lasting legacy. His reign saw a flourishing of Mughal art and architecture, blending Persian, Indian, and Islamic styles. Notable architectural achievements of his era include the construction of the Humayun's Tomb in Delhi, the Agra Fort, and the magnificent city of Fatehpur Sikri. Fatehpur Sikri, with its grand palaces, mosques, and public buildings, remains a testament to Akbar's architectural vision and the cultural fusion that characterized his reign.

The Mughal court under Akbar was a center of cultural and intellectual activity. He patronized poets, artists, and scholars, and his reign saw the compilation of important literary works, including the Ain-i-Akbari and the Akbarnama by his court historian Abul Fazl.

These texts provide invaluable insights into the administration, culture, and daily life of the Mughal Empire.

Akbar's reign also had a significant impact on the economy and trade. His policies promoted internal trade and commerce, and he encouraged the growth of handicrafts and industries. The establishment of a standardized currency facilitated trade, and the empire's extensive network of roads and communication systems enhanced connectivity. Akbar's diplomatic relations with foreign powers, including the Ottoman Empire, Persia, and European nations, further boosted trade and cultural exchanges.

Despite his achievements, Akbar's reign was not without challenges. He faced several rebellions and opposition from orthodox Muslim clerics who were critical of his liberal religious policies. However, his ability to navigate these challenges and maintain the loyalty of his subjects through a combination of diplomacy, military prowess, and administrative efficiency underscored his exceptional leadership qualities.

Akbar's personal life was as dynamic as his political career. He married several times, forming alliances with various Rajput and other noble families. His marriages to Rajput princesses, including Jodha Bai, fostered goodwill and loyalty among the Rajputs. Akbar's harem was diverse, reflecting the multicultural nature of his court.

In his later years, Akbar's focus shifted towards consolidating and administering his vast empire. He continued to promote policies that encouraged cultural integration and economic prosperity. His legacy was carried forward by his successors, particularly his son Jahangir and grandson Shah Jahan, who inherited a stable and prosperous empire.

Akbar's death on October 27, 1605, marked the end of an era. He was buried in a grand mausoleum in Sikandra, near Agra, a site that continues to attract visitors from around the world. Akbar's reign left an indelible mark on Indian history, shaping the social, cultural, and political landscape of the subcontinent.

Chapter 36: Queen Mary of Scots

Mary, Queen of Scots, born on December 8, 1542, in Linlithgow Palace, Scotland, was one of the most intriguing and tragic figures in British history. Her life was marked by dramatic personal and political upheavals, religious conflict, and ultimately, imprisonment and execution. She became Queen of Scotland when she was just six days old, following the death of her father, James V of Scotland. Her tumultuous life, filled with power struggles, alliances, marriages, and betrayals, has captured the imagination of historians and the public alike.

Mary Stuart, as she was also known, was the only surviving legitimate child of King James V of Scotland and his French wife, Mary of Guise. With her father's death occurring so shortly after her birth, Mary became queen in infancy, and the regency was initially held by her mother. As a Catholic queen in a predominantly Protestant Scotland, her reign was fraught with religious tension from the outset.

In 1548, at the age of five, Mary was sent to France for her safety and to secure a dynastic alliance with the powerful French monarchy. She was betrothed to the Dauphin Francis, the heir to the French throne, as part of the Treaty of Haddington. During her years in France, Mary received an exceptional education, becoming fluent in French, Latin, Spanish, and Italian, and she was trained in the refined manners and cultural pursuits of the French court. Her time in France was marked by a close bond with the royal family, and she was known for her beauty, intelligence, and charm.

In 1558, Mary married the Dauphin, who became King Francis II of France the following year. As queen consort of France, Mary enjoyed a brief period of influence and power. However, Francis's reign was short-lived; he died in 1560, leaving Mary a widow at the age of 18. With her mother's death that same year, Mary decided to return to

Scotland, a country she had left as a child and one that had undergone significant religious and political changes during her absence.

Mary returned to a Scotland divided by the Reformation. The Protestant Reformation, led by figures such as John Knox, had taken a strong hold in Scotland, creating a volatile environment for a Catholic monarch. Despite these challenges, Mary initially sought to rule with a degree of religious tolerance. She allowed the Protestant Church to continue while maintaining her Catholic faith, hoping to unite her divided subjects.

In 1565, Mary married her first cousin, Henry Stuart, Lord Darnley. The union was partly driven by the need to strengthen her claim to the English throne. Darnley himself had a claim to the English crown through his mother, a granddaughter of Henry VII of England. However, the marriage quickly soured due to Darnley's arrogance, ambition, and erratic behavior. The couple's relationship deteriorated, exacerbated by political intrigue and mutual distrust.

The birth of their son, James VI of Scotland and future James I of England, in 1566, briefly united Mary and Darnley. However, tensions remained high, culminating in the mysterious murder of Darnley in 1567. He was found strangled in the garden of Kirk o' Field, a house in Edinburgh, after an explosion had destroyed the building. Suspicion fell on several nobles, including James Hepburn, Earl of Bothwell, who was widely believed to have orchestrated the murder.

In a controversial and fateful decision, Mary married Bothwell just three months after Darnley's death. This marriage was scandalous and widely condemned, leading to a rapid loss of support among the Scottish nobility. Many believed that Bothwell had abducted and possibly raped Mary to coerce her into marriage, though the true nature of their relationship remains unclear. The marriage triggered a rebellion led by disaffected nobles, resulting in Mary's capture and forced abdication in favor of her infant son, James VI.

Mary fled to England in 1568, seeking the protection of her cousin, Queen Elizabeth I. However, Elizabeth saw Mary as a significant threat due to her strong claim to the English throne and her Catholic faith, which made her a figurehead for Catholic plots against Elizabeth. Consequently, Mary was imprisoned by Elizabeth for nearly 19 years. During her imprisonment, Mary became the focus of numerous Catholic conspiracies aiming to dethrone Elizabeth and place Mary on the English throne. The most notable of these was the Babington Plot of 1586, which sought to assassinate Elizabeth and incite a Catholic uprising.

Elizabeth's government, led by her spymaster Sir Francis Walsingham, uncovered the Babington Plot through intercepted letters between Mary and the conspirators. This discovery provided the evidence needed to charge Mary with treason. She was tried and found guilty in a politically charged trial. Despite Elizabeth's initial reluctance to execute a fellow monarch, the pressure from her advisors and the perceived threat to her life led to Mary's execution.

On February 8, 1587, Mary, Queen of Scots, was beheaded at Fotheringhay Castle. Her execution was a somber and dignified affair, reflecting her royal status and her devout Catholic faith. Dressed in a red petticoat, symbolizing martyrdom, Mary faced her death with composure. Her execution marked the end of a life filled with drama and tragedy but also solidified her legacy as a martyr for the Catholic cause and a romanticized figure in history and literature.

Mary's death had significant political ramifications. It removed a major Catholic threat to Elizabeth's reign but also heightened tensions between England and Catholic powers, particularly Spain. The execution of a Catholic queen further alienated Catholic subjects in England and Scotland and contributed to the deteriorating relationship with Spain, leading to the attempted invasion by the Spanish Armada in 1588.

In retrospect, Mary, Queen of Scots, remains a complex and enigmatic figure. Her life and reign were shaped by the turbulent religious and political landscape of 16th-century Europe. Despite her tragic end, Mary's legacy endured through her son, James VI of Scotland, who succeeded Elizabeth I as James I of England, uniting the crowns of England and Scotland. This dynastic union laid the foundation for the future United Kingdom.

Mary's life has inspired countless works of literature, drama, and film, cementing her place in popular culture as a symbol of tragic beauty, doomed ambition, and the relentless pursuit of power. Her story continues to captivate historians and the public alike, offering a poignant reflection on the complexities of power, religion, and personal fate in the early modern period.

Chapter 37: King Philip II of Spain

King Philip II of Spain, born on May 21, 1527, in Valladolid, Spain, was one of the most powerful and influential monarchs of the 16th century. His reign, spanning from 1556 to 1598, marked a period of immense territorial expansion, intense religious conflict, and significant political and cultural developments. As the ruler of the Spanish Empire, Philip II oversaw vast territories in Europe, the Americas, Asia, and Africa, and his efforts to consolidate and defend his empire had far-reaching consequences for global history.

Philip was the son of Holy Roman Emperor Charles V and Isabella of Portugal. He was raised in a court that was both intensely religious and politically astute, receiving an education that emphasized statesmanship, languages, and military strategy. From an early age, Philip was groomed to inherit his father's vast dominions, and he quickly demonstrated a keen aptitude for governance and diplomacy.

In 1554, Philip married Mary I of England, forming a political alliance aimed at strengthening Catholic influence in Europe. Although the marriage was short-lived due to Mary's death in 1558, it had significant implications. Philip became King of England and Ireland through his marriage, although his power was limited by English law and the will of his wife. The marriage did not produce any heirs, and with Mary's death, Philip's direct influence over English affairs ended, although his involvement in English politics would continue to be significant.

Philip's ascension to the Spanish throne in 1556 marked the beginning of a reign characterized by both immense power and numerous challenges. One of his primary goals was to consolidate and centralize the various territories under his control. This included not only the kingdoms of Spain and Portugal but also the Netherlands, parts of Italy, and vast overseas territories in the Americas and Asia. Philip sought to strengthen royal authority and reduce the power of local nobles and regional parliaments, a policy that often led to resistance and rebellion.

One of the most significant challenges Philip faced was the Revolt of the Netherlands. The Dutch provinces, predominantly Protestant and economically prosperous, resented the heavy taxation and religious persecution imposed by the Catholic Spanish administration. The revolt, which began in 1566, quickly escalated into a protracted and bloody conflict. Philip's attempts to crush the rebellion through military force and harsh measures, such as the Council of Troubles (nicknamed the "Council of Blood"), only fueled resistance. The revolt eventually led to the independence of the northern provinces, which formed the Dutch Republic in 1581, although the southern provinces remained under Spanish control.

Philip's reign was also marked by his staunch commitment to defending and promoting Catholicism, both within his realms and across Europe. This religious zeal was a driving force behind many of his policies and conflicts. Philip saw himself as the protector of the Catholic faith against the rising tide of Protestantism, and his efforts to suppress heresy were relentless. This included support for the Spanish Inquisition, which sought to root out and punish heresy within his dominions.

One of the most notable examples of Philip's commitment to Catholicism was his involvement in the Battle of Lepanto in 1571. This naval battle, fought between the Holy League (a coalition of Catholic states) and the Ottoman Empire, was a decisive victory for the Christian forces and a significant check on Ottoman expansion in the Mediterranean. The victory at Lepanto was celebrated across Catholic Europe and solidified Philip's reputation as a defender of the faith.

Philip's foreign policy was heavily influenced by his desire to counter Protestant influence and expand Catholic power. This included conflicts with Protestant England and support for Catholic factions in the French Wars of Religion. One of the most famous episodes of his reign was the attempted invasion of England in 1588, known as the Spanish Armada. Philip sought to overthrow the Protestant Queen Elizabeth I and restore Catholicism to England. However, the Armada met with disaster, largely due to unfavorable weather conditions and the strategic prowess of the English navy. The defeat of the Spanish Armada was a significant setback for Philip and marked a turning point in the decline of Spanish naval dominance.

Despite these setbacks, Philip's reign saw significant achievements in other areas. His administration implemented a range of economic and administrative reforms aimed at improving the efficiency and stability of the Spanish Empire. This included efforts to streamline the bureaucracy, enhance tax collection, and promote economic development. Philip also oversaw the completion of the Escorial, a vast palace and monastery complex near Madrid that served as a symbol of his power and piety.

Philip's overseas empire continued to expand during his reign, with significant territorial gains in the Americas and Asia. Spanish explorers and conquistadors established new colonies and trade routes, bringing immense wealth to the Spanish crown through the extraction of silver and other resources. However, the influx of wealth also led to economic challenges, including inflation and overreliance on American silver, which would have long-term implications for the Spanish economy.

In the latter part of his reign, Philip faced increasing challenges, both domestically and internationally. The ongoing conflict in the Netherlands drained resources and weakened Spanish influence in northern Europe. Additionally, the strain of continuous warfare and the cost of maintaining a vast empire took a toll on the Spanish treasury. Philip's efforts to centralize authority and impose religious uniformity often led to resistance and unrest, further complicating his rule.

Philip's personal life was marked by a series of marriages and the succession of his children. He was married four times: to Maria

Manuela of Portugal, Mary I of England, Elisabeth of Valois, and Anna of Austria. These marriages were primarily political alliances aimed at strengthening Spain's position in Europe. Philip's heir, Philip III, succeeded him upon his death in 1598, inheriting a vast but troubled empire.

Philip II's legacy is complex and multifaceted. He was a ruler who wielded immense power and left a lasting impact on the course of European and global history. His efforts to consolidate and defend his empire, promote Catholicism, and expand Spanish influence were significant, but they also led to prolonged conflicts, economic challenges, and eventual decline. Philip's reign was characterized by both remarkable achievements and notable failures, reflecting the complexities and contradictions of his era.

Philip II's impact extended beyond his lifetime, shaping the future of Spain and its global empire. His policies and conflicts influenced the course of European history, contributing to the rise of Protestant powers and the gradual decline of Spanish dominance. The cultural and architectural achievements of his reign, including the construction of the Escorial and the flourishing of the Spanish Renaissance, left a lasting legacy on Spanish culture and heritage.

Chapter 38: King James I of England

King James I of England, also known as James VI of Scotland, was born on June 19, 1566, at Edinburgh Castle, Scotland. He was the son of Mary, Queen of Scots, and her second husband, Henry Stuart, Lord Darnley. James's early life was marked by political turmoil, including his mother's forced abdication and imprisonment, and he became King of Scotland at just 13 months old following her abdication in 1567. Under the regency of several noble lords, James's upbringing was influenced by the Protestant faith, which played a significant role in shaping his worldview and policies.

James's reign as King of Scotland was characterized by efforts to consolidate royal authority and promote religious unity in a country deeply divided by sectarian tensions between Catholics and Protestants. He pursued a policy of conciliation towards both religious factions, seeking to establish a moderate form of Protestantism as the official religion while granting limited tolerance to Catholics. This approach, known as the "Golden Age" of Scottish history, helped to stabilize the kingdom and lay the groundwork for James's eventual succession to the English throne.

In 1603, following the death of Queen Elizabeth I of England, James inherited the English crown, becoming the first monarch to rule over both England and Scotland. His accession to the English throne marked the beginning of the Stuart dynasty's rule in England and the end of the Tudor era. The union of the English and Scottish crowns under James ushered in a period of relative stability and cultural flourishing known as the Jacobean era.

As King of England, James faced numerous challenges, including religious conflicts, financial difficulties, and tensions with Parliament. One of the most significant religious issues of his reign was the ongoing conflict between Catholics and Protestants. Despite his efforts to promote religious tolerance, James's policies often favored the

Protestant majority, leading to increased persecution of Catholics and tensions within the realm.

James's relationship with Parliament was also contentious, particularly regarding issues of taxation and royal prerogative. His belief in the divine right of kings clashed with Parliament's desire for greater political power and representation. This tension came to a head with the Gunpowder Plot of 1605, a failed Catholic conspiracy to assassinate James and blow up the Houses of Parliament. The plot, orchestrated by the Catholic conspirator Guy Fawkes, resulted in severe repression of Catholics and further strained relations between the monarchy and Parliament.

Despite these challenges, James's reign was marked by significant cultural achievements and advancements. He was a patron of the arts and literature, presiding over a vibrant cultural scene that included the works of playwrights such as William Shakespeare, Ben Jonson, and John Donne. James himself was a prolific writer, producing several works on topics ranging from theology and politics to witchcraft and tobacco.

One of James's most enduring legacies is the Authorized King James Version of the Bible, first published in 1611. Commissioned by James to create a new English translation of the Bible, the King James Version became one of the most widely read and influential translations in the history of Christianity, shaping the English language and religious thought for centuries to come.

James's personal life was also tumultuous, marked by political intrigue and scandal. He was married to Anne of Denmark, with whom he had several children, including future King Charles I. James's relationships with his wife and courtiers were often fraught, and rumors of his alleged homosexuality and extramarital affairs circulated throughout his reign.

In terms of foreign policy, James pursued a policy of peace and diplomacy, seeking to avoid costly and protracted conflicts with

England's European rivals. He negotiated treaties with Spain and the Netherlands, attempting to maintain a balance of power on the continent while focusing on domestic matters. However, James's efforts to avoid war were not always successful, and England became embroiled in several conflicts during his reign, including the Thirty Years' War and conflicts with Spain over control of the Spanish Netherlands.

James's reign came to an end with his death on March 27, 1625, at Theobalds House in Hertfordshire, England. He was succeeded by his son Charles I, whose reign would be marked by even greater political and religious turmoil, ultimately leading to the English Civil War and the execution of Charles I in 1649.

Chapter 39: Emperor Shah Jahan of India

Emperor Shah Jahan, born Khurram on January 5, 1592, in Lahore, Mughal Empire (present-day Pakistan), was one of the most illustrious rulers of the Mughal dynasty in India. He ascended to the throne in 1628 after a protracted succession struggle, succeeding his father, Jahangir, as the fifth emperor of the Mughal Empire. Shah Jahan's reign is often referred to as the "Golden Age" of the Mughal Empire, characterized by remarkable cultural achievements, architectural splendor, and political stability.

Shah Jahan's early years were marked by exposure to the arts, literature, and military training, instilling in him a deep appreciation for culture and warfare. He received a comprehensive education under the guidance of renowned scholars and mentors, becoming proficient in various languages, including Persian, Arabic, and Turkish. His military training equipped him with the skills necessary to lead armies and govern a vast and diverse empire.

One of the defining features of Shah Jahan's reign was his patronage of the arts and architecture, which reached unprecedented heights during his rule. He was a passionate connoisseur of art and literature, fostering a rich cultural environment at his court. Under his patronage, the Mughal court became a center of artistic excellence, attracting poets, scholars, musicians, and artists from across the empire and beyond.

Shah Jahan's most enduring legacy is undoubtedly the construction of the Taj Mahal, one of the most iconic and celebrated monuments in the world. Commissioned in 1632 as a mausoleum for his beloved wife, Mumtaz Mahal, who died during childbirth, the Taj Mahal stands as a testament to Shah Jahan's love and devotion. Built over a period of 22 years by thousands of artisans and craftsmen, the Taj Mahal is renowned for its breathtaking beauty, intricate marble carvings, and symmetrical design. It is considered a masterpiece of Mughal architecture and a symbol of enduring love.

In addition to the Taj Mahal, Shah Jahan commissioned numerous other architectural marvels, including the Red Fort in Delhi, the Jama Masjid in Delhi, the Shalimar Gardens in Lahore, and the Shah Jahan Mosque in Thatta. These grand structures reflected the emperor's vision of grandeur and splendor, serving as symbols of his power and magnificence. They also contributed to the cultural and architectural legacy of the Mughal Empire, influencing subsequent generations of architects and builders.

Shah Jahan's reign was also marked by significant military achievements and territorial expansion. He waged several successful military campaigns to assert Mughal dominance over various regions of the Indian subcontinent, extending the empire's boundaries and consolidating its power. His conquests included the subjugation of the Deccan Sultanates, the annexation of the kingdoms of Golconda and Bijapur, and the suppression of rebellions in Bengal and Rajasthan.

Despite his military successes, Shah Jahan's reign was not without challenges. He faced internal revolts, external threats from neighboring powers, and occasional conflict with his own sons over succession. One of the most notable challenges came from his son Aurangzeb, who rebelled against his father and ultimately seized power in 1658, leading to Shah Jahan's imprisonment.

In 1657, Shah Jahan fell seriously ill, leading to a power struggle among his sons for the throne. Aurangzeb emerged victorious and declared himself emperor after defeating his brothers in a series of battles. Shah Jahan was deposed and imprisoned in the Agra Fort, where he spent the remaining years of his life under house arrest. Despite his confinement, Shah Jahan continued to receive the respect and reverence befitting a former emperor, and he remained a figure of considerable influence within the empire.

During his captivity, Shah Jahan devoted himself to religious contemplation and artistic pursuits, continuing to commission works of art and poetry. He also maintained correspondence with scholars, poets, and administrators, offering guidance and advice on matters of state. Despite his physical isolation, Shah Jahan remained deeply engaged in the affairs of the empire until his death on January 22, 1666.

Chapter 40: King Charles I of England

King Charles I of England, born on November 19, 1600, at Dunfermline Palace in Scotland, was the second son of King James VI of Scotland (later James I of England) and Anne of Denmark. Charles's ascension to the throne in 1625 marked the beginning of a tumultuous period in English history, culminating in the English Civil War and his eventual execution in 1649. His reign was characterized by conflicts with Parliament, religious tensions, and challenges to royal authority, ultimately leading to the overthrow of the monarchy and the establishment of the Commonwealth under Oliver Cromwell.

Charles's early years were shaped by his upbringing in the Stuart court, where he received a comprehensive education in politics, theology, and the arts. Despite his reserved and introverted nature, Charles was groomed for kingship and demonstrated a strong belief in the divine right of kings, a doctrine that asserted the king's absolute authority and accountability to God alone.

Upon his accession to the throne in 1625, Charles faced a series of political and religious challenges that would define his reign. One of the most pressing issues was the conflict with Parliament over taxation and the extent of royal prerogative. Parliament, led by figures such as Sir John Eliot and John Pym, sought to limit the king's power and assert its own authority over matters of taxation and governance. Charles, however, believed firmly in the royal prerogative and resisted Parliament's attempts to encroach upon his authority.

Religious tensions also simmered beneath the surface of Charles's reign, exacerbated by his marriage to Henrietta Maria of France, a devout Catholic. Charles's attempts to promote religious tolerance and grant concessions to Catholics alienated many Protestants, who viewed Catholicism with suspicion and fear. The king's religious policies, combined with his authoritarian style of governance, contributed to growing discontent and division within the realm.

One of the most contentious issues of Charles's reign was his attempt to impose religious conformity in Scotland by introducing a new Book of Common Prayer. This decision sparked widespread opposition and resistance among the Scottish clergy and laity, culminating in the signing of the National Covenant in 1638, a document affirming the Presbyterian faith and rejecting royal interference in church affairs. The ensuing conflict, known as the Bishops' Wars, resulted in military defeats for Charles and further strained his relationship with Parliament.

Charles's inability to govern effectively without the support of Parliament led to a series of political crises and confrontations. In 1629, he dissolved Parliament and ruled without it for over a decade, a period known as the Personal Rule or the Eleven Years Tyranny. During this time, Charles relied heavily on royal prerogative and unpopular measures such as Ship Money, a tax levied on coastal towns to fund the navy. These actions fueled resentment and opposition to the king's rule, laying the groundwork for the subsequent civil war.

In 1640, Charles was forced to recall Parliament due to financial difficulties and the outbreak of rebellion in Scotland. The convening of the Long Parliament marked a turning point in Charles's reign, as Parliament seized the opportunity to assert its authority and demand concessions from the king. Tensions between the king and Parliament escalated rapidly, leading to a breakdown in relations and the outbreak of civil war in 1642.

The English Civil War pitted the Royalists, loyal to the king, against the Parliamentarians, who sought to curtail royal power and establish a constitutional monarchy. Despite early successes, including the capture of London and victory at the Battle of Edgehill, Charles's fortunes waned as the war dragged on. The decisive turning point came with the defeat of the Royalist forces at the Battle of Naseby in 1645, after which Parliament gained the upper hand.

In 1646, Charles surrendered to the Scottish army, hoping to negotiate a settlement with the Covenanters. However, he soon found himself at odds with the Scottish Parliament, which handed him over to the English Parliament in exchange for financial compensation. Charles's imprisonment marked the beginning of a protracted political and legal struggle between the king and his opponents over the terms of his trial and the nature of his authority.

In January 1649, Charles was tried by a specially constituted court, the High Court of Justice, on charges of high treason and other offenses against the state. Despite his defiant defense and refusal to recognize the court's jurisdiction, Charles was found guilty and sentenced to death by execution. On January 30, 1649, he was beheaded outside the Banqueting House in Whitehall, London, in front of a large crowd of spectators.

The execution of King Charles I shocked Europe and sent shockwaves throughout the English-speaking world. It marked the first time in English history that a reigning monarch had been tried and executed by his own subjects, signaling the end of absolute monarchy and the beginning of a new era of republican government. Charles's death also laid the foundation for the establishment of the Commonwealth under Oliver Cromwell and the eventual restoration of the monarchy under his son, Charles II, in 1660.

Chapter 41: King Louis XIV of France

King Louis XIV of France, born on September 5, 1638, in the Château de Saint-Germain-en-Laye, was one of the longest-reigning monarchs in European history and is often referred to as the "Sun King." His reign, which lasted from 1643 until his death in 1715, was marked by a remarkable centralization of power, cultural splendor, and military conquests that transformed France into the dominant European power of the 17th century.

Louis XIV ascended to the throne at the age of four following the death of his father, King Louis XIII, making him one of the youngest monarchs in French history. During his minority, France was ruled by a regency council led by his mother, Anne of Austria, and the chief minister, Cardinal Mazarin. The early years of Louis's reign were marked by political instability and conflict, including the Fronde, a series of uprisings against royal authority by nobles and parlements seeking to limit the power of the monarchy.

As he reached adulthood, Louis XIV sought to assert his authority and establish himself as an absolute monarch. He viewed himself as the embodiment of divine right and believed that his authority came directly from God. In 1661, Louis took personal control of the government following the death of Cardinal Mazarin, inaugurating a period of personal rule known as the "reign of the king's personal government."

Louis XIV's reign was characterized by his relentless pursuit of centralization and consolidation of power. He sought to curb the influence of the nobility and establish the supremacy of the monarchy over all aspects of French life. One of the key instruments of his rule was the system of absolute monarchy, in which the king's word was law and his authority was unchecked by any other institution. Louis famously declared, "L'État, c'est moi" ("I am the state"), encapsulating his vision of kingship as synonymous with the state itself.

To reinforce his authority, Louis XIV established a highly centralized system of government with himself at the center. He appointed loyal officials and administrators to key positions of power, bypassing traditional aristocratic channels of influence. He also established a vast bureaucracy to administer the affairs of state, with ministries responsible for finance, war, justice, and foreign affairs. The king's court at Versailles served as the seat of government and the center of political and cultural life in France, where nobles competed for royal favor and the king's attention.

Louis XIV's reign was also marked by his ambitious building projects and patronage of the arts. He transformed the modest hunting lodge of Versailles into a magnificent palace that served as a symbol of his power and grandeur. Designed by architects such as Louis Le Vau and Jules Hardouin-Mansart, Versailles became the epitome of Baroque architecture and the center of courtly life in France. The palace was adorned with lavish furnishings, sumptuous gardens, and works of art commissioned by the king to glorify his reign.

The arts flourished under Louis XIV's patronage, with France becoming a leading center of culture and refinement in Europe. The king supported artists, writers, and musicians, including playwrights such as Molière and Racine, composers such as Jean-Baptiste Lully, and painters such as Charles Le Brun. These artists produced works that celebrated the glory of the monarchy and promoted the values of classical order and harmony.

Louis XIV's reign was also marked by military conquests and expansionist ambitions. He waged a series of wars aimed at extending French influence and securing its borders, including the War of Devolution, the Dutch War, the War of the Reunions, and the War of the Spanish Succession. These conflicts brought France into conflict with its European neighbors and resulted in territorial gains, but they also imposed a heavy burden on the French economy and society.

Louis XIV's foreign policy was guided by the principles of raison d'état (reason of state) and gloire (glory), which emphasized the pursuit of national interest and the projection of French power. He sought to establish France as the preeminent European power and to assert its cultural, political, and military dominance on the continent. However, his aggressive expansionism and interventions in the affairs of neighboring states provoked resentment and opposition, leading to a series of coalitions against France and ultimately to the War of the Spanish Succession.

In his later years, Louis XIV faced growing challenges and crises, including economic hardship, famine, and popular discontent. The costs of war and grandiose building projects strained the royal treasury and exacerbated social inequalities. The king's absolutist rule also engendered opposition from within the nobility and clergy, who resented his centralization of power and encroachment on their privileges.

Louis XIV died on September 1, 1715, after a reign of 72 years, making him the longest-reigning monarch in European history up to that point. His death marked the end of an era and the beginning of a period of transition and upheaval in France. Despite his achievements as a patron of the arts and a promoter of French power and prestige, Louis XIV's absolutist rule and imperial ambitions left a legacy of centralized authority and militarism that would shape the course of French history for centuries to come.

Chapter 42: Queen Anne of England

Queen Anne, born on February 6, 1665, was the last monarch of the Stuart dynasty and reigned as Queen of England, Scotland, and Ireland from March 8, 1702, until her death on August 1, 1714. Her reign was a significant period in English history, marked by political and religious upheaval, military conflict, and the consolidation of parliamentary power.

Anne was the second daughter of King James II and his first wife, Anne Hyde. Her early life was marked by political turmoil, including the Glorious Revolution of 1688, which led to the deposition of her father and the accession of her Protestant sister, Mary II, and her husband, William III, to the throne. Anne's own succession to the throne in 1702 followed the deaths of William III and Mary II, who had no surviving children.

Anne's reign was characterized by the emergence of political parties, the growth of parliamentary power, and significant developments in domestic and foreign policy. As a constitutional monarch, Anne was bound by the principles of parliamentary sovereignty and limited monarchy, which had been established during the Glorious Revolution. Throughout her reign, she worked closely with her ministers and Parliament to govern the realm and enact legislation.

One of the most notable aspects of Anne's reign was her involvement in the War of the Spanish Succession, a major European conflict fought between 1701 and 1714 over the succession to the Spanish throne. Anne's government supported the Grand Alliance, a coalition of European powers opposed to the prospect of a single Bourbon monarch ruling both France and Spain, which would upset the balance of power in Europe. The war saw significant military engagements, including the Battle of Blenheim in 1704, where British forces under the command of John Churchill, Duke of Marlborough, achieved a decisive victory over the French and Bavarian armies.

The War of the Spanish Succession had far-reaching consequences for England and Europe, shaping the geopolitical landscape and influencing the balance of power on the continent. Anne's support for the Grand Alliance contributed to the eventual defeat of the Bourbon powers and the signing of the Treaty of Utrecht in 1713, which brought an end to the war and secured significant territorial gains for Britain, including Gibraltar and Minorca.

In addition to her role in the War of the Spanish Succession, Anne's reign saw significant developments in domestic policy and religious affairs. She presided over the Act of Union in 1707, which united the kingdoms of England and Scotland to form the Kingdom of Great Britain, creating a single parliament and government for the entire island. The union was intended to strengthen British unity and security and to promote economic and social integration between the two kingdoms.

Anne's reign also saw the passage of important legislation, including the Act of Settlement in 1701, which established the Protestant succession to the throne and excluded Catholics from the line of succession. This legislation was a response to the perceived threat of Catholicism and Jacobitism, which sought to restore the Stuart dynasty to the throne.

Anne's personal life was marked by tragedy and loss. Despite her marriage to Prince George of Denmark in 1683, Anne experienced numerous miscarriages and stillbirths, and none of her children survived infancy. This lack of a direct heir to the throne contributed to the instability of the succession and fueled political tensions and intrigues during her reign.

Anne's health also deteriorated in her later years, and she suffered from various illnesses, including gout and obesity. Her declining health and the absence of a clear heir to the throne prompted political maneuvering and factionalism within the royal court and among the leading political figures of the day.

Queen Anne died on August 1, 1714, at Kensington Palace, ending a reign of over 12 years. She was succeeded by her second cousin, George of Hanover, who became King George I of Great Britain, marking the beginning of the Hanoverian dynasty. Despite the challenges and controversies of her reign, Anne is remembered as a conscientious and dutiful monarch who presided over a period of significant change and transformation in English and European history. Her reign witnessed the consolidation of parliamentary power, the expansion of British influence abroad, and the emergence of Britain as a major European power in its own right.

Chapter 43: Emperor Peter the Great of Russia

Emperor Peter I of Russia, commonly known as Peter the Great, was born on June 9, 1672, in Moscow, to Tsar Alexis I and his second wife, Natalya Naryshkina. Peter's reign, which lasted from 1682 until his death in 1725, marked a pivotal era in Russian history. He is best known for his extensive efforts to modernize Russia and transform it into a major European power through comprehensive administrative, military, economic, and cultural reforms. His legacy is characterized by the dramatic changes he brought to Russian society, governance, and international standing.

Peter's early life was shaped by the political turmoil and factionalism of the Russian court. Following his father's death in 1676, Peter's half-brother, Feodor III, ascended to the throne. Upon Feodor's death in 1682, a power struggle ensued between the Naryshkin family, to which Peter belonged, and the Miloslavsky family, representing the interests of his half-brother Ivan. This conflict culminated in the Moscow Uprising of 1682, during which Peter witnessed the brutal violence that claimed the lives of many of his relatives. Eventually, a compromise was reached, and Peter was declared co-tsar alongside Ivan V, with their sister Sophia acting as regent.

During Sophia's regency, Peter was largely kept away from the political center in Moscow and resided in the village of Preobrazhenskoye, where he indulged his interest in military affairs by organizing mock battles and forming regiments composed of his playmates and local youths. These experiences laid the groundwork for his later military reforms. Peter's curiosity and desire for learning led him to seek knowledge from foreign experts and to immerse himself in the study of shipbuilding, navigation, and other technical skills.

In 1689, Peter, with the support of his loyal followers, successfully staged a coup against Sophia, leading to her removal from power. Ivan V remained a titular co-ruler until his death in 1696, after which Peter became the sole ruler of Russia. With his authority consolidated, Peter embarked on a series of ambitious reforms aimed at transforming Russia into a modern state.

One of Peter's primary goals was to strengthen and modernize the Russian military. He sought to build a powerful navy to secure Russia's access to the seas and to compete with the maritime powers of Western Europe. In 1697, Peter embarked on the Grand Embassy, a diplomatic mission to Western Europe, during which he traveled incognito under the alias "Peter Mikhailov." The Grand Embassy was a formative experience for Peter; he studied shipbuilding in the Dutch Republic, observed military practices in Prussia, and gained insights into the administrative and technological advancements of Western Europe. This journey reinforced his conviction that Russia needed to adopt Western methods to become a formidable power.

Upon his return to Russia in 1698, Peter implemented sweeping military reforms. He established the Russian Navy, building shipyards and commissioning warships to assert Russian naval power. The construction of a modern navy was critical for Peter's ambitions to expand Russian influence, particularly in the Baltic Sea and the Black Sea. Peter also restructured the army, introducing new training methods, tactics, and Western-style uniforms. He established the Preobrazhensky and Semyonovsky Guards regiments, which became the elite units of the Russian military.

Peter's military ambitions led to the Great Northern War (1700–1721), a protracted conflict against the Swedish Empire, which was then a dominant power in Northern Europe. The war began disastrously for Russia with a crushing defeat at the Battle of Narva in 1700. Undeterred, Peter reorganized his forces and implemented further military reforms. The turning point came with the Battle of

Poltava in 1709, where Peter's forces decisively defeated the Swedish army, leading to a significant shift in the balance of power in the region. The war culminated in the Treaty of Nystad in 1721, which granted Russia significant territorial gains, including access to the Baltic Sea, thus fulfilling Peter's strategic objectives and marking the emergence of Russia as a major European power.

Parallel to his military reforms, Peter undertook extensive administrative and governmental changes to centralize and streamline the Russian state. He introduced the Table of Ranks in 1722, a system that classified the nobility and civil servants into fourteen ranks, based on merit rather than heredity. This system aimed to create a meritocratic bureaucracy, reduce the power of the traditional aristocracy, and ensure loyalty to the state. Peter also established a Senate to oversee the administration of the empire, replacing the outdated Boyar Duma. The Senate was responsible for legislative, judicial, and financial matters, acting as the highest governing body in Peter's absence.

Peter's drive for modernization extended to the economy. He sought to diversify and strengthen Russia's economic base by encouraging the development of new industries, such as textiles, mining, and metallurgy. He promoted the establishment of factories and workshops, often staffed by foreign experts and skilled laborers. Peter also reformed the tax system, introducing new taxes and improving tax collection methods to fund his ambitious projects and military campaigns. His economic policies were aimed at increasing state revenue and reducing Russia's reliance on foreign imports.

One of Peter's most ambitious projects was the founding of a new capital, St. Petersburg, in 1703. Situated on the Baltic Sea, St. Petersburg was intended to be a "window to the West" and a symbol of Russia's new orientation towards Europe. The construction of the city was a monumental undertaking, involving massive labor and resources. Despite the harsh climate and challenging conditions, St. Petersburg quickly grew into a major cultural and administrative center. The city's layout and architecture reflected Peter's admiration for Western European styles, and it became a hub for commerce, industry, and the arts.

Peter's cultural and educational reforms were also significant. He sought to Westernize Russian society by introducing Western customs, clothing, and manners. He established schools and academies to provide education in the sciences, engineering, and navigation, aiming to create a skilled and knowledgeable populace capable of supporting his modernization efforts. The establishment of the Russian Academy of Sciences in 1724 was a testament to Peter's commitment to fostering scientific and intellectual advancement.

Peter's reforms extended to the church as well. He sought to reduce the power of the Russian Orthodox Church and bring it under state control. In 1721, he abolished the office of the Patriarch, the highest ecclesiastical authority in the Russian Orthodox Church, and replaced it with the Holy Synod, a government body composed of bishops and lay officials. This move ensured that the church would serve the interests of the state and further consolidated Peter's control over all aspects of Russian life.

Despite his many achievements, Peter's reign was not without controversy and opposition. His reforms were often implemented with harsh measures and met with resistance from various segments of society, including the traditional nobility, the clergy, and the peasantry. Peter's policies of forced Westernization and modernization disrupted established customs and practices, leading to social tensions and unrest. The Streltsy Uprising of 1698, an attempt by the elite military corps to restore traditional power structures, was brutally suppressed by Peter, exemplifying his ruthless approach to dissent.

Peter's personal life was marked by tragedy and complexity. His first marriage to Eudoxia Lopukhina was unhappy and ended in separation. Their son, Alexei, became a focal point of conflict between father and son. Alexei opposed many of Peter's reforms and sought to undermine his father's authority. In 1718, Alexei was arrested, tried for treason, and ultimately sentenced to death, although he died under mysterious circumstances before the execution could take place. This event left a profound impact on Peter and underscored the personal sacrifices he made in pursuit of his vision for Russia.

In his later years, Peter continued to focus on consolidating his reforms and ensuring the stability of the empire. He faced health issues, likely exacerbated by the rigorous lifestyle he led and the injuries sustained during his military campaigns. Peter died on February 8, 1725, in St. Petersburg. His death marked the end of an era, but his legacy endured through the profound changes he brought to Russia.

Peter the Great's reign fundamentally transformed Russia, propelling it onto the world stage as a major European power. His military victories and territorial expansions secured Russia's strategic interests and enhanced its influence. His administrative, economic, and cultural reforms modernized Russian society and governance, laying the foundation for the future development of the Russian state. Peter's efforts to Westernize Russia and integrate it into the broader European context had a lasting impact, shaping the trajectory of Russian history for centuries to come.

Historians have long debated Peter's legacy, with some viewing him as a visionary reformer who brought Russia out of medieval stagnation and into modernity, while others criticize his authoritarian methods and the social costs of his reforms. Regardless of these differing perspectives, Peter the Great remains one of the most significant figures in Russian history, a ruler whose ambition, vision, and determination reshaped his nation and left an indelible mark on the world. His reign is a testament to the complexities and challenges of state-building and modernization, and his legacy continues to be studied and admired for its enduring impact on the course of history.

Chapter 44: Emperor Frederick II of Prussia

Emperor Frederick II of Prussia, commonly known as Frederick the Great, was born on January 24, 1712, in Berlin. He was the eldest son of Frederick William I of Prussia, known as the "Soldier King," and Sophia Dorothea of Hanover. His reign, from 1740 until his death in 1786, marked a transformative period in Prussian history. Frederick II is remembered for his military brilliance, administrative reforms, patronage of the arts and sciences, and his embodiment of the principles of enlightened absolutism.

Frederick's early life was heavily influenced by the strict and militaristic upbringing imposed by his father. Frederick William I was a severe disciplinarian who instilled in his son the values of frugality, discipline, and military prowess. However, young Frederick had a more artistic and intellectual inclination, showing interest in literature, philosophy, and music. He secretly corresponded with French Enlightenment thinkers like Voltaire and aspired to a life that combined intellectual pursuits with statecraft. This created a significant rift between father and son, culminating in Frederick's attempted escape to England in 1730, which led to his arrest and the execution of his friend and co-conspirator, Hans Hermann von Katte.

Despite this tumultuous relationship, Frederick eventually embraced his role as the heir to the throne. Upon his father's death in 1740, he ascended to the throne as King of Prussia. One of his first acts as king was to defy the Pragmatic Sanction, which sought to secure the Habsburg succession through Maria Theresa, and invade Silesia, a prosperous province. This action precipitated the War of the Austrian Succession (1740–1748), during which Frederick displayed remarkable military acumen. His victories at the battles of Mollwitz

(1741) and Chotusitz (1742) secured Silesia for Prussia, significantly expanding its territory and prestige.

The annexation of Silesia marked the beginning of Frederick's military and political strategies aimed at enhancing Prussia's power and influence. Frederick's military campaigns are characterized by their strategic brilliance, innovative tactics, and effective use of limited resources. His concept of "oblique order" in battle, where he focused his forces on a decisive point to break enemy lines, became a hallmark of his military genius. Frederick's successes on the battlefield earned him the moniker "Frederick the Great."

Frederick's reign saw the consolidation of Prussian power through a series of wars and diplomatic maneuvers. The most significant of these conflicts was the Seven Years' War (1756–1763), a global conflict that pitted Prussia and Britain against a coalition of France, Austria, Russia, and Sweden. Despite being vastly outnumbered and facing invasions from multiple fronts, Frederick managed to secure several key victories, including the battles of Rossbach (1757) and Leuthen (1757). His resilience and tactical genius during this war elevated Prussia to the status of a major European power. The Treaty of Hubertusburg (1763) concluded the war, confirming Prussia's possession of Silesia and cementing Frederick's reputation as one of the greatest military leaders of his time.

Beyond his military achievements, Frederick the Great is also celebrated for his enlightened absolutism and administrative reforms. Influenced by the ideas of the Enlightenment, Frederick sought to modernize and rationalize the administration of his kingdom. He introduced legal reforms aimed at standardizing and codifying Prussian law, reducing the influence of arbitrary rule, and ensuring a more efficient and equitable justice system. The General Code of Prussian Law, although completed after his death, was initiated under his reign and reflected his commitment to legal rationality.

Frederick also implemented significant economic reforms. He promoted agricultural development by encouraging the cultivation of new crops, such as potatoes, and improving irrigation systems. His policies aimed at increasing agricultural productivity and ensuring food security for his subjects. Additionally, Frederick supported the development of industries, trade, and infrastructure, recognizing the importance of economic stability and growth in strengthening the state.

Education and culture were other areas where Frederick left a lasting impact. He founded the Berlin Academy of Sciences and fostered an environment where intellectual and cultural pursuits could thrive. Frederick himself was an accomplished flutist and composed several musical pieces. His patronage of the arts extended to architecture as well; he commissioned the construction of numerous buildings, including the Rococo masterpiece Sanssouci Palace in Potsdam, which became his favorite residence and a symbol of his reign.

Frederick's enlightened absolutism extended to his religious policies as well. He promoted religious tolerance and sought to minimize the influence of the clergy on state affairs. His famous dictum, "In my kingdom, everyone can go to heaven in his own fashion," exemplified his pragmatic approach to religion. While he was a devout Calvinist in public, Frederick maintained a personal skepticism towards organized religion and sought to ensure that religious differences did not impede the functioning of the state.

Frederick's foreign policy was characterized by his strategic acumen and diplomatic finesse. He skillfully navigated the complex web of European alliances, balancing relationships with major powers to Prussia's advantage. His diplomatic efforts were aimed at maintaining the balance of power in Europe, preventing any single state from becoming overwhelmingly dominant. Frederick's ability to engage in both military and diplomatic maneuvers earned him respect and admiration from contemporaries and later historians alike.

Despite his numerous achievements, Frederick's reign was not without challenges and criticisms. His aggressive military campaigns and expansionist policies often led to significant human and economic costs. The harsh discipline he imposed on his soldiers and the burdens of prolonged warfare took a toll on Prussian society. Additionally, Frederick's reliance on a highly centralized and autocratic system of governance meant that he often ruled with little regard for the opinions of his subjects or advisors.

Frederick's personal life also contributed to his complex legacy. His relationship with his family, particularly with his father and his own wife, Elisabeth Christine of Brunswick-Wolfenbüttel-Bevern, was strained and distant. Frederick and Elisabeth lived largely separate lives, and he showed little interest in her after their marriage, focusing instead on his intellectual and military pursuits. His close relationships with male companions, such as Hans Hermann von Katte and his later confidant, the Marquis de la Valfons, have led some historians to speculate about his sexuality, although definitive evidence remains elusive.

Frederick the Great's later years were marked by a combination of continued reform efforts and reflections on his legacy. He remained active in governance until his death, overseeing the administration of his kingdom and engaging in intellectual pursuits. His writings, including his "Anti-Machiavel," which critiqued Machiavellian principles of power, and his numerous essays on military strategy, philosophy, and statecraft, offer insights into his thoughts and the principles that guided his reign.

Frederick died on August 17, 1786, at Sanssouci Palace, leaving behind a transformed Prussia that had emerged as a significant European power. His impact on the military, administrative, and cultural development of Prussia was profound, and his legacy continued to influence subsequent generations of rulers and statesmen. The reforms he implemented and the principles of enlightened absolutism he espoused laid the groundwork for the modernization of the Prussian state and its eventual unification with other German territories.

Historians have long debated Frederick's legacy, with some viewing him as a progressive and enlightened ruler who advanced the cause of rational governance and others criticizing him as a ruthless autocrat whose military ambitions brought immense suffering. Regardless of these differing perspectives, Frederick the Great remains an iconic figure in European history, whose life and reign exemplify the complexities and contradictions of enlightened absolutism.

Chapter 45: Queen Maria Theresa of Austria

Queen Maria Theresa of Austria, born on May 13, 1717, in Vienna, was a pivotal figure in European history. As the only female ruler of the Habsburg dominions and the last of the House of Habsburg, her reign marked a significant era of reforms, wars, and political machinations. Her tenure as the sovereign of Austria, Hungary, and Bohemia from 1740 to 1780 saw profound changes that reshaped the contours of the Habsburg Empire, setting the stage for the modern European state system.

Maria Theresa was the eldest daughter of Emperor Charles VI and Elisabeth Christine of Brunswick-Wolfenbüttel. Her birth came during a period when the Habsburg dynasty was deeply concerned about securing a male heir. When it became clear that Charles VI would have no male offspring, he promulgated the Pragmatic Sanction of 1713. This decree aimed to ensure that his hereditary lands could be inherited by a daughter, thus preserving the Habsburg territories intact.

Maria Theresa's upbringing was carefully tailored to prepare her for potential rulership. She received a comprehensive education that included languages, history, and political theory, but it was steeped in the traditional values of the Habsburg dynasty. Despite this preparation, many contemporaries doubted her capacity to govern, primarily due to prevailing gender biases of the era.

Upon her father's death in 1740, Maria Theresa ascended to the throne amid a flurry of diplomatic and military challenges. The War of the Austrian Succession (1740-1748) erupted almost immediately, as various European powers contested her right to rule. Key opponents included Prussia, led by Frederick the Great, and France, both of whom sought to capitalize on the perceived vulnerability of a female sovereign. The war saw the loss of the rich province of Silesia to Prussia, a blow that deeply affected Maria Theresa but also steeled her resolve to strengthen her empire.

Despite initial setbacks, Maria Theresa demonstrated remarkable political and military acumen. She rallied support from Britain, the Dutch Republic, and other European powers, ultimately securing her position through the Treaty of Aix-la-Chapelle in 1748. The war underscored the necessity of reforming the Habsburg military and administrative apparatus, spurring a series of extensive changes that would define her reign.

One of Maria Theresa's most significant achievements was her comprehensive program of internal reforms, aimed at modernizing and centralizing the Habsburg administration. She established a more efficient tax system, which improved the financial stability of the empire. The centralization efforts included the creation of a standing army, a significant shift from the previously decentralized and feudal levies that had characterized Habsburg military forces. These reforms were instrumental in transforming the Habsburg dominions into a more cohesive and powerful state.

Maria Theresa also focused on improving the legal and educational systems. She codified laws, making the legal system more transparent and accessible. Her educational reforms were particularly noteworthy. She mandated compulsory primary education for both boys and girls, a pioneering move that laid the groundwork for modern public education in the Habsburg lands. This initiative not only improved literacy rates but also fostered a sense of shared identity and loyalty to the state.

Religious policy was another area where Maria Theresa left a lasting impact. As a devout Catholic, she sought to strengthen the influence of the Church while also implementing measures to control and supervise its activities. Her policies often walked a fine line between fostering religious unity and limiting the power of the clergy. Notably, she took steps to curb the influence of the Jesuits, whom she viewed as too powerful and independent, culminating in the suppression of the order in 1773.

Maria Theresa's reign also witnessed significant economic reforms. She promoted agricultural innovation and industrial development, seeking to enhance the empire's economic resilience. The introduction of new crops, such as the potato, and improvements in farming techniques helped to boost agricultural productivity. Additionally, she encouraged the establishment of manufactories and trade, aiming to reduce the empire's dependence on imports and stimulate domestic production.

Foreign policy during Maria Theresa's reign was dominated by the rivalry with Prussia and the quest to reclaim Silesia. This rivalry culminated in the Seven Years' War (1756-1763), a global conflict that saw alliances shift and expand beyond Europe. Despite substantial efforts and considerable losses, Maria Theresa was unable to reclaim Silesia from Frederick the Great. However, the war reaffirmed her resolve to maintain and strengthen her empire's international standing.

One of the more personal and strategic aspects of Maria Theresa's reign was her use of marriage alliances to secure her dynasty's future. She married Francis Stephen of Lorraine, who later became Holy Roman Emperor Francis I. Their union produced sixteen children, many of whom she strategically married off to cement alliances across Europe. The most famous of these children was Marie Antoinette, who became the queen consort of Louis XVI of France. These marriages, often referred to as the "Diplomatic Marriages," were a key element of Maria Theresa's foreign policy, designed to secure the Habsburgs' influence and create a network of powerful alliances.

Maria Theresa's personality and leadership style were marked by a blend of pragmatism, determination, and maternalism. She was known for her hands-on approach to governance, often involving herself directly in administrative and policy matters. Her correspondence reveals a ruler deeply concerned with the welfare of her subjects and the stability of her empire. She combined traditional monarchical authority with an enlightened approach to governance, which earned her respect both within her empire and among contemporary rulers.

Her relationship with her children was complex and often strategic. She groomed her eldest son, Joseph II, for leadership, involving him in state affairs from an early age. However, their differing views on governance led to frequent tensions. Joseph, who succeeded her as Holy Roman Emperor, was more radical in his reformist zeal, often clashing with his mother's more cautious and pragmatic approach. Despite these differences, Maria Theresa's influence on Joseph and her other children was profound, shaping their views on governance and statecraft.

The final years of Maria Theresa's reign were marked by consolidation and continued reform. She worked tirelessly to strengthen her empire, addressing issues such as serfdom and judicial corruption. Her health began to decline in the late 1770s, and she passed away on November 29, 1780, in Vienna. Her death marked the end of an era but left a legacy that would endure long after.

Maria Theresa's reign had a lasting impact on the Habsburg Empire and Europe as a whole. Her reforms laid the foundation for a more centralized and efficient state, capable of competing with the other great powers of Europe. Her emphasis on education and legal reform contributed to the development of a more enlightened and progressive society. Despite the challenges and conflicts of her reign, Maria Theresa is remembered as a formidable and capable ruler who navigated the complexities of her time with skill and determination.

Historians often view Maria Theresa as a pioneering female monarch whose reign bridged the gap between traditional monarchical rule and the emerging ideals of the Enlightenment. Her ability to balance these competing influences and implement meaningful reforms has cemented her place as one of the most significant figures in

European history. Her legacy continues to be studied and admired for its impact on the shaping of modern statecraft and governance.

197

Chapter 46: Catherine the Great of Russia

Catherine the Great, born Sophie Friederike Auguste von Anhalt-Zerbst on May 2, 1729, in Stettin, Prussia (now Szczecin, Poland), was one of the most remarkable and influential rulers of Russia. Her reign, which lasted from 1762 until her death in 1796, is often regarded as the Golden Age of the Russian Empire. Catherine's tenure saw significant territorial expansion, internal reform, and the flourishing of Russian culture and arts, firmly establishing her legacy as one of the most formidable female monarchs in history.

Sophie was born to a minor German princely family. Her father, Christian August, Prince of Anhalt-Zerbst, was a military officer in the Prussian army, and her mother, Johanna Elisabeth of Holstein-Gottorp, was an ambitious woman who aspired to see her daughter marry into a prominent royal family. Sophie's early education was comprehensive, covering subjects such as French, which was the language of the European aristocracy, as well as literature, history, and philosophy. This education would later serve her well as an enlightened ruler.

In 1744, Sophie was selected as the bride for the future Tsar Peter III of Russia, largely due to the efforts of Empress Elizabeth of Russia, who sought to strengthen ties with German states. Upon her arrival in Russia, Sophie converted to Eastern Orthodoxy, adopting the name Catherine (Ekaterina) and learning the Russian language. Her marriage to Peter, however, was fraught with difficulties. Peter was immature, erratic, and unpopular with the Russian court and military, which only served to highlight Catherine's intelligence, political acumen, and adaptability.

Peter III ascended to the throne in January 1762 following the death of Empress Elizabeth. His brief reign was marked by erratic policies and alienation of the powerful Russian nobility and military. His pro-Prussian stance and attempts to modernize the army along Prussian lines further isolated him. Sensing an opportunity, Catherine garnered support among the military and political elite. In a coup d'état in July 1762, Peter was deposed, and Catherine was proclaimed Empress of Russia. Peter was subsequently imprisoned and died under mysterious circumstances, which many believe was orchestrated by Catherine's supporters.

Catherine's reign began with the aim of modernizing and strengthening Russia, drawing inspiration from the Enlightenment. She corresponded with prominent philosophers such as Voltaire, Diderot, and d'Alembert, embracing their ideas on governance, education, and law. One of her early initiatives was the drafting of a new legal code, the Nakaz (Instruction), which was intended to guide the Legislative Commission convened in 1767. The Nakaz drew heavily on Enlightenment principles, advocating for the protection of personal liberty, the elimination of torture, and the establishment of equality before the law. Although the commission did not achieve its goals, the Nakaz demonstrated Catherine's commitment to reform and legal modernization.

Catherine's domestic policies focused on centralizing power and strengthening the autocracy. She reorganized the provincial administration, dividing Russia into fifty provinces, each governed by appointed officials responsible for law enforcement, tax collection, and public welfare. This reform aimed to improve the efficiency of governance and reduce corruption. Additionally, Catherine promoted economic development by encouraging the establishment of new industries, improving infrastructure, and granting incentives to foreign entrepreneurs and skilled workers to settle in Russia.

Education was another area where Catherine sought to make significant changes. Recognizing the importance of education in fostering an enlightened and productive citizenry, she founded the

Smolny Institute in 1764, the first state-funded school for girls in Russia. She also supported the establishment of secular schools and universities, promoting a curriculum that included sciences, mathematics, and modern languages. Catherine's emphasis on education extended to the arts and culture, where she was a patron of literature, music, and theater, contributing to the cultural enrichment of Russian society.

Catherine's reign was also marked by significant territorial expansion. She continued the policies of her predecessors in extending Russian influence and control over neighboring territories. One of her most notable achievements was the annexation of Crimea in 1783, which secured Russian access to the Black Sea and was a strategic victory over the Ottoman Empire. Her military successes against the Ottomans in the Russo-Turkish Wars (1768–1774 and 1787–1792) further solidified Russian dominance in the region, leading to the Treaty of Küçük Kaynarca, which granted Russia significant territorial gains and the right to protect Orthodox Christians within the Ottoman Empire.

In the west, Catherine capitalized on the political instability in Poland-Lithuania. Through a series of partitions in 1772, 1793, and 1795, orchestrated in collaboration with Prussia and Austria, Poland was effectively divided and absorbed into these empires, erasing Poland from the map of Europe for over a century. These partitions expanded Russian territory significantly, bringing large populations of Poles, Lithuanians, and other ethnic groups under Russian rule.

Catherine's reign was not without challenges and controversies. The Pugachev Rebellion (1773–1775), led by the Cossack Emelyan Pugachev, was a major peasant uprising that threatened her rule. Claiming to be the deceased Peter III, Pugachev rallied discontented peasants, serfs, and Cossacks with promises of land and freedom from serfdom. The rebellion was brutally suppressed by Catherine's forces, but it exposed the deep social and economic divides in Russian society.

In response, Catherine implemented measures to strengthen serfdom, increasing the nobility's control over their serfs and consolidating her support among the aristocracy.

Despite her enlightened rhetoric, Catherine's policies towards the serfs and her reliance on the nobility for support demonstrated the limitations of her reforms. Her reign saw the consolidation of serfdom, with serfs facing increased exploitation and restrictions on their mobility. This tension between her enlightened ideals and the realities of maintaining autocratic power underscored the complexities of her rule.

Catherine's personal life was as eventful as her political career. Her numerous relationships with influential men, including military leaders, politicians, and artists, were well-known. Many of her lovers, such as Grigory Orlov and Grigory Potemkin, played significant roles in her court and government, often wielding considerable influence. Potemkin, in particular, was a close confidant and advisor, contributing to military and administrative reforms and the colonization of newly acquired territories.

Catherine's later years were marked by increasing conservatism, as she sought to maintain stability and control in the face of growing revolutionary sentiments across Europe. The French Revolution, which began in 1789, alarmed Catherine, leading her to suppress any signs of dissent within Russia and to support conservative forces in Europe. Her reaction to the revolution highlighted her pragmatic approach to governance, prioritizing the preservation of her own power and the existing social order over ideological consistency.

Catherine the Great died on November 17, 1796, leaving behind a legacy of profound transformation and expansion in Russia. Her reign had elevated Russia to the status of a major European power, with a significantly enlarged territory and a more centralized and efficient administrative system. Culturally, she had fostered a period of enlightenment and artistic flourishing, establishing institutions that would have lasting impacts on Russian society.

Catherine's contributions to Russian history are multifaceted. She is celebrated for her enlightened reforms, her patronage of the arts, and her successful military campaigns. However, her reign also exemplified the tensions between autocratic rule and the ideals of the Enlightenment, as well as the challenges of implementing meaningful social change in a deeply hierarchical society. Catherine the Great remains one of the most compelling and influential figures in Russian history, a ruler whose ambition, intelligence, and vision left an indelible mark on the nation and the world.

Chapter 47: King Louis XVI of France

King Louis XVI of France, born Louis-Auguste on August 23, 1754, at the Palace of Versailles, was the last reigning monarch of France before the French Revolution overthrew the monarchy. His reign, from 1774 until his execution in 1793, was marked by financial crises, political turmoil, and revolutionary fervor. Louis XVI's inability to navigate these challenges led to the downfall of the French monarchy and his own tragic end.

Louis-Auguste was the third son of Louis, Dauphin of France, and Maria Josepha of Saxony. His early life was relatively unremarkable, as he was not initially expected to ascend to the throne. However, the deaths of his elder brothers placed him directly in line for succession. Known for his shy and reserved nature, Louis was not seen as a strong or decisive figure, traits that would later prove detrimental during his reign.

Educated by private tutors, Louis was well-versed in history, geography, and languages but lacked the practical experience and political acumen necessary for effective leadership. His interest in locksmithing and other hobbies often overshadowed his engagement with state affairs. At the age of 15, he married the Austrian archduchess Marie Antoinette, a union meant to solidify the alliance between France and Austria. The marriage was initially unpopular among the French people, who viewed it as a political maneuver rather than a genuine partnership.

Louis XVI ascended to the throne on May 10, 1774, following the death of his grandfather, King Louis XV. France was already facing significant financial difficulties due to prolonged involvement in costly wars, including the Seven Years' War. The country's fiscal woes were exacerbated by a tax system that disproportionately burdened the common people while the nobility and clergy enjoyed numerous exemptions.

Louis XVI inherited a kingdom in dire need of reform, but his indecisiveness and lack of strong leadership hindered effective solutions. He appointed a series of finance ministers, including Jacques Turgot, Jacques Necker, and Charles Alexandre de Calonne, each of whom proposed various reforms to stabilize the economy. Turgot's attempts to reduce government spending and introduce new taxes met with resistance from the privileged classes, leading to his dismissal. Necker, more popular among the public, implemented measures to increase transparency in royal finances but faced opposition from the court. Calonne's proposal to impose a universal land tax failed to gain traction, highlighting the deep-seated resistance to change among the French elite.

The financial crisis reached a critical point in the late 1780s, forcing Louis XVI to convene the Estates-General in 1789. This assembly, which had not been called since 1614, comprised representatives from the three estates: the clergy, the nobility, and the commoners. The Third Estate, representing the commoners, was determined to address the inequities of the Ancien Régime. Their grievances and demands for representation led to the formation of the National Assembly, marking the beginning of the French Revolution.

Louis XVI's handling of the Estates-General and the subsequent National Assembly demonstrated his inability to effectively manage the growing unrest. Initially attempting to placate the Third Estate, he later resorted to resistance and obstruction. The situation escalated with the storming of the Bastille on July 14, 1789, a symbol of the monarchy's oppression. This event galvanized revolutionary fervor and marked a turning point in the revolution.

In an attempt to regain control, Louis XVI accepted the National Assembly's decrees, including the Declaration of the Rights of Man and of the Citizen, which enshrined principles of equality, liberty, and popular sovereignty. However, his acceptance was perceived as insincere, and his perceived vacillation further eroded his authority.

The Women's March on Versailles in October 1789 forced the royal family to relocate to the Tuileries Palace in Paris, effectively placing them under the control of the revolutionaries.

The relationship between the king and the revolutionaries deteriorated further when Louis XVI attempted to flee Paris with his family in June 1791. The royal family's capture in Varennes and subsequent return to Paris fueled suspicions of the king's loyalty to the revolutionary cause. This event, known as the Flight to Varennes, was a significant turning point that diminished the king's credibility and increased calls for the abolition of the monarchy.

In 1792, France declared war on Austria, and the resulting conflict intensified internal divisions. The radical Jacobins, led by figures like Maximilien Robespierre and Georges Danton, gained prominence, advocating for the establishment of a republic. The growing radicalism culminated in the storming of the Tuileries Palace on August 10, 1792, leading to the suspension of the monarchy and the imprisonment of the royal family.

Louis XVI's trial began in December 1792, with the National Convention, now the governing body, acting as the jury. Accused of high treason and conspiracy against the state, Louis faced a politically charged trial. The evidence presented against him included his correspondence with foreign powers and his actions perceived as undermining the revolution. Despite his defense, the Convention found him guilty. On January 21, 1793, Louis XVI was executed by guillotine in the Place de la Révolution, marking the end of more than a thousand years of continuous French monarchy.

Louis XVI's reign is often viewed through the lens of his failures and the revolutionary upheaval that followed. His inability to implement meaningful reforms and navigate the complex political landscape contributed to the monarchy's downfall. However, some historians argue that Louis was a well-intentioned but ill-equipped ruler, facing insurmountable challenges in a period of unprecedented change.

The legacy of Louis XVI is intertwined with the broader context of the French Revolution, a transformative period that reshaped France and had a lasting impact on the world. The revolution introduced radical ideas about governance, citizenship, and human rights that would influence subsequent democratic movements. While Louis XVI's reign ended in tragedy, his life and the revolution that overthrew him remain subjects of extensive study and reflection, highlighting the complexities of leadership and the profound consequences of political and social upheaval.

Chapter 48: Napoleon Bonaparte

Napoleon Bonaparte, born on August 15, 1769, in Ajaccio, Corsica, was a military genius and a towering figure in European history. His life was marked by extraordinary achievements and significant controversy, embodying the tumultuous era of the French Revolution and the Napoleonic Wars. As the Emperor of the French, he profoundly influenced the political landscape of Europe, leaving a legacy that continues to be studied and debated.

Napoleon was born into a minor noble family of Italian descent. His father, Carlo Buonaparte, was an attorney and a political figure in Corsica. His mother, Letizia Ramolino, was known for her strict discipline and strong will, traits that Napoleon would inherit. He was the second of eight surviving children. When he was nine, Napoleon was sent to mainland France to attend military school, first at Brienne-le-Château and later at the prestigious École Militaire in Paris. Despite initially facing prejudice as an outsider and non-native French speaker, he excelled in his studies, particularly in mathematics and military science, graduating as a second lieutenant of artillery at the age of 16.

The French Revolution, which began in 1789, provided the backdrop for Napoleon's rise to power. The revolution overthrew the old monarchy and established a republic, but it also plunged France into chaos and conflict. Napoleon, aligning himself with the revolutionary cause, rapidly advanced through the military ranks. His first major opportunity came in 1793 during the Siege of Toulon, where he played a crucial role in retaking the city from royalist forces, earning a promotion to brigadier general.

In 1795, Napoleon helped suppress a royalist uprising in Paris, an action that further enhanced his reputation. His success caught the attention of the Directory, the ruling government of France, which appointed him commander of the Army of Italy. During the Italian campaign of 1796-1797, Napoleon demonstrated his strategic brilliance, winning a series of decisive battles against Austrian forces and expanding French influence in the region. These victories not only secured his military reputation but also brought him immense wealth and political clout.

Napoleon's ambition extended beyond the battlefield. In 1798, he led an expedition to Egypt, aiming to disrupt British trade routes to India and establish a French presence in the Middle East. The campaign included the famous Battle of the Pyramids, where Napoleon's forces defeated the Mamluks. However, the French fleet was later destroyed by the British at the Battle of the Nile, stranding Napoleon and his army. Despite the military setbacks, the Egyptian campaign was notable for its scientific and cultural impact, including the discovery of the Rosetta Stone, which would later be crucial in deciphering Egyptian hieroglyphs.

By 1799, France was in political turmoil, with the Directory losing control and the country facing threats from both external and internal enemies. Sensing an opportunity, Napoleon returned to France and participated in a coup d'état on November 9, 1799 (18 Brumaire), overthrowing the Directory and establishing the Consulate. Napoleon became First Consul, effectively becoming the ruler of France. He initiated a series of reforms aimed at stabilizing the country, including the centralization of administrative control, the establishment of the Bank of France, and the creation of the Napoleonic Code, a comprehensive set of civil laws that would have a lasting influence on legal systems worldwide.

In 1804, Napoleon crowned himself Emperor of the French, an act that both solidified his power and marked the return of monarchical rule in a republic born out of revolution. This period of his reign is characterized by a series of military campaigns, collectively known as the Napoleonic Wars, aimed at expanding French hegemony across Europe. His Grand Armée won numerous battles, including the Battle of Austerlitz in 1805, often regarded as his greatest victory, where he decisively defeated the combined forces of Austria and Russia.

However, Napoleon's aggressive expansionism also led to the formation of coalitions against him, drawing much of Europe into prolonged conflict. His invasion of Russia in 1812 marked a turning point. The campaign initially saw French forces advancing deep into Russian territory, but the harsh winter, logistical failures, and staunch Russian resistance led to a catastrophic retreat, decimating the Grand Armée. This defeat emboldened Napoleon's enemies, leading to the formation of the Sixth Coalition, which eventually forced his abdication in 1814.

Exiled to the island of Elba, Napoleon's time away from power was short-lived. In 1815, he escaped and returned to France, rallying support and reclaiming his throne in a period known as the Hundred Days. His return sparked renewed conflict, culminating in the Battle of Waterloo on June 18, 1815, where British and Prussian forces decisively defeated him. This defeat marked the end of his rule and led to his second abdication.

Napoleon was subsequently exiled to the remote island of Saint Helena in the South Atlantic Ocean, where he spent the remaining years of his life. During his exile, he dictated his memoirs, reflecting on his life and achievements. He died on May 5, 1821, under circumstances that have sparked various theories, though the official cause of death was stomach cancer.

Napoleon's impact on Europe and the world was profound and multifaceted. Militarily, he revolutionized warfare with his use of mass conscription, rapid maneuvering, and the integration of different arms of the military into cohesive units. His strategies and tactics are still studied in military academies around the world. Politically, he reshaped the map of Europe, spreading the principles of the French Revolution, including meritocracy, legal equality, and the abolition of feudal privileges, albeit often enforced through authoritarian means.

The Napoleonic Code, one of his most enduring legacies, influenced legal systems far beyond France. It established clear and accessible laws that emphasized individual rights, property rights, and secular authority. Many of its principles are still in use today in various legal systems, particularly in Europe and Latin America.

Culturally, Napoleon's reign saw the promotion of the arts and sciences. He supported institutions such as the Louvre, which he transformed into a world-class museum. His patronage extended to education and public works, including the construction of roads, bridges, and monuments, many of which still stand today as testaments to his ambition.

Napoleon's life and career remain subjects of intense study and debate. He is often seen as a complex figure who combined visionary leadership with ruthless ambition. His ability to inspire and lead, coupled with his relentless pursuit of power, has made him a legendary figure in history. Critics argue that his quest for dominance led to unnecessary wars and suffering, while admirers praise his reforms and military genius.

In France, Napoleon's legacy is particularly contentious. He is remembered both as a national hero who restored stability and as a tyrant who betrayed the revolutionary ideals. His tomb at Les Invalides in Paris is a site of national pride and reflection.

Internationally, Napoleon's influence extended far beyond Europe. His actions indirectly contributed to the independence movements in Latin America and the spread of nationalist ideas. His legacy also includes the rise of military leaders and statesmen who sought to emulate his successes and learn from his failures.

Napoleon Bonaparte's life was a remarkable journey from the relatively obscure beginnings on the island of Corsica to the height of imperial power and ultimately to exile and death on a remote island. His story is a testament to the heights of human ambition and the dramatic shifts of fortune that can accompany it. Napoleon remains a towering figure in history, whose legacy continues to shape the modern world in myriad ways.

Chapter 49: Queen Victoria of the United Kingdom

Queen Victoria, born Alexandrina Victoria on May 24, 1819, at Kensington Palace in London, was the only child of Prince Edward, Duke of Kent and Strathearn, and Princess Victoria of Saxe-Coburg-Saalfeld. Her father died when she was just eight months old, and her mother raised her under strict supervision, following the so-called Kensington System, a set of rigid protocols designed to keep her dependent and isolated. This upbringing fostered a deep sense of duty and a formidable determination, traits that would characterize her reign.

Victoria ascended to the throne on June 20, 1837, following the death of her uncle, King William IV. At just 18 years old, she became queen of the United Kingdom of Great Britain and Ireland. Her early reign was influenced by her first Prime Minister, Lord Melbourne, who became her trusted advisor and political mentor. Their close relationship helped Victoria navigate the complexities of her new role and provided her with a sense of stability and guidance.

In 1840, Victoria married her first cousin, Prince Albert of Saxe-Coburg and Gotha. The marriage was both a love match and a political alliance, and the couple had nine children. Albert played a significant role in Victoria's life and reign, advising her on political and diplomatic matters and championing a range of social reforms. He was instrumental in the organization of the Great Exhibition of 1851, a showcase of industrial innovation and a symbol of Britain's leading role in the Industrial Revolution.

Victoria's marriage to Albert was marked by deep affection and mutual respect, and his death in 1861 devastated her. Overcome with grief, she withdrew from public life for many years, wearing black mourning attire and rarely appearing in public. This period of seclusion led to criticism and a temporary decline in the monarchy's popularity. However, her eventual return to public duties helped to restore her standing and reaffirm the monarchy's place in British society.

The Victorian era, named after Queen Victoria, was a time of profound change and progress. It was marked by the Industrial Revolution, which transformed the British economy and society. Advances in technology, transportation, and communication revolutionized daily life. The expansion of the railway network, the invention of the telegraph, and the rise of factories and mass production all contributed to unprecedented economic growth and urbanization.

Victoria's reign also saw significant political and social reforms. The Reform Act of 1832, which preceded her accession, had already begun the process of expanding the electorate. Subsequent reforms during her reign, including the Second Reform Act of 1867 and the Representation of the People Act of 1884, further extended voting rights and democratized the political system. The introduction of these reforms reflected the changing attitudes towards governance and the growing influence of the middle and working classes.

Throughout her reign, Victoria's relationship with her prime ministers was pivotal in shaping her legacy. She worked with numerous prime ministers, including notable figures such as Sir Robert Peel, Benjamin Disraeli, and William Ewart Gladstone. Her rapport with Disraeli was particularly warm, as he flattered and supported her, whereas her relationship with Gladstone was more strained due to their differing political views and his more formal demeanor.

Victoria's role as the head of a growing British Empire was another defining aspect of her reign. Under her rule, the British Empire expanded to its zenith, becoming the largest empire in history. This expansion was driven by both economic interests and a belief in the civilizing mission of imperialism. The acquisition of territories in Africa, Asia, and the Pacific enhanced Britain's global influence and brought immense wealth, but it also involved exploitation and conflict. Victoria herself took an active interest in imperial affairs, and in 1876, she was proclaimed Empress of India, symbolizing the crown's dominance over the subcontinent.

The Victorian era was also a time of cultural flourishing. Literature, art, and science all advanced significantly. Authors such as Charles Dickens, the Brontë sisters, and Thomas Hardy captured the complexities of Victorian society in their works. The Pre-Raphaelite Brotherhood and other artists sought to challenge conventional artistic norms, while scientists like Charles Darwin revolutionized understanding of the natural world with his theory of evolution. These cultural and intellectual developments reflected the dynamic and often contradictory nature of Victorian Britain.

Despite her conservative views, Victoria's long reign witnessed the gradual improvement of social conditions and the rise of the welfare state. The Factory Acts, which regulated working conditions, the Public Health Acts, which addressed urban sanitation, and the Education Act of 1870, which laid the groundwork for compulsory schooling, were all enacted during her reign. These reforms, although limited in scope, marked the beginning of a broader movement towards social justice and the protection of the vulnerable.

Victoria's later years were marked by a resurgence in her popularity and a renewed sense of public engagement. Her Golden Jubilee in 1887 and Diamond Jubilee in 1897 were celebrated with great enthusiasm, reflecting her status as a beloved figurehead of the British nation and empire. These jubilees were not only occasions for national celebration but also opportunities to display the unity and strength of the British Empire.

In her final years, Victoria continued to play an active role in state affairs, despite her advancing age and declining health. She maintained a close interest in her family, which had become known as the "grandmother of Europe" due to the strategic marriages of her children and grandchildren into various European royal families. This network of alliances helped to maintain peace in Europe, although it also contributed to the complex web of relations that eventually led to World War I.

Queen Victoria died on January 22, 1901, at Osborne House on the Isle of Wight. Her death marked the end of an era and the beginning of the Edwardian period under her son and successor, King Edward VII. Her passing was mourned by millions, and her funeral was a grand state occasion that reflected her stature and the respect she commanded.

Victoria's legacy is vast and complex. She presided over a period of unprecedented change and left an indelible mark on British and world history. Her reign saw the transformation of Britain into a modern industrial nation and the expansion of the British Empire to its greatest extent. She was a symbol of stability and continuity in a rapidly changing world, and her influence extended far beyond the borders of her own country.

Victoria's personal qualities, including her sense of duty, her resilience in the face of personal tragedy, and her ability to adapt to changing circumstances, endeared her to her subjects and ensured her place in history as one of Britain's greatest monarchs. Her reign encapsulated the spirit of the age and left a lasting legacy that continues to be felt to this day.

Chapter 50: Queen Elizabeth II of the United Kingdom

Queen Elizabeth II, born Elizabeth Alexandra Mary Windsor on April 21, 1926, in London, was the longest-reigning monarch in British history, serving as the queen of the United Kingdom and other Commonwealth realms from February 6, 1952, until her death on September 8, 2022. Her reign spanned seven decades, witnessing significant social, political, and technological transformations.

Elizabeth was the first child of the Duke and Duchess of York, who later became King George VI and Queen Elizabeth. Her birth, during the reign of her grandfather, King George V, placed her third in the line of succession, behind her uncle, Edward, Prince of Wales, and her father. She was educated privately at home and developed a strong sense of duty and dedication to public service early on.

Her life took a dramatic turn in 1936 when her grandfather died, and her uncle ascended the throne as King Edward VIII. However, his abdication later that year to marry Wallis Simpson, a twice-divorced American socialite, unexpectedly placed her father on the throne as King George VI. This event propelled Elizabeth into the position of heir presumptive, fundamentally changing her life's trajectory.

During World War II, Elizabeth and her sister, Princess Margaret, were evacuated to Windsor Castle to avoid the Blitz. In 1945, at the age of 19, she insisted on joining the Auxiliary Territorial Service, where she trained as a driver and mechanic, becoming the first female member of the royal family to serve in the military.

Elizabeth married Lieutenant Philip Mountbatten, a former prince of Greece and Denmark, on November 20, 1947. The wedding was a much-needed morale boost for a nation recovering from the ravages of war. Philip, who became Duke of Edinburgh, supported Elizabeth throughout her reign. They had four children: Charles, Anne, Andrew, and Edward.

Her father's health deteriorated in the early 1950s, and Elizabeth increasingly took on more public duties. While on a tour of Kenya in February 1952, she received the news of her father's death, marking the beginning of her reign. She was just 25 years old. Her coronation on June 2, 1953, was the first to be televised, drawing a global audience and marking the beginning of a new era in which the monarchy became more accessible to the public.

Throughout her reign, Queen Elizabeth II was known for her steadfast dedication to her role. She navigated a changing world with a deep sense of duty and a commitment to the principles of constitutional monarchy. Her reign saw the decolonization of Africa and the Caribbean, the United Kingdom's entry into and later departure from the European Union, and significant social changes within the UK and the Commonwealth.

One of the defining aspects of her reign was her relationship with successive prime ministers. From Winston Churchill to Liz Truss, she worked with 15 prime ministers, offering counsel and stability. Her regular audiences with prime ministers were a key aspect of her role, allowing her to stay informed about national affairs and provide her perspective shaped by decades of experience.

Elizabeth's reign was also marked by numerous royal tours and state visits. She was the most widely traveled head of state in history, visiting over 100 countries and playing a crucial role in strengthening diplomatic ties. Her visits often had significant political and symbolic importance, such as her historic state visit to the Republic of Ireland in 2011, which helped to improve Anglo-Irish relations.

The Queen was a patron of over 600 charities and organizations, reflecting her deep commitment to public service. She was particularly interested in issues related to education, health, and the welfare of veterans and the armed forces. Her dedication to these causes helped to raise awareness and funds, benefiting countless individuals and communities.

Her personal life, though often kept private, was not without its challenges and controversies. The breakdown of the marriages of three of her children in the 1990s, particularly the very public separation and subsequent death of Princess Diana, tested the monarchy's resilience and public image. The Queen's handling of these crises, including her measured response to Diana's death, was crucial in maintaining the monarchy's stability and relevance.

In her later years, Elizabeth II faced further challenges, including the scrutiny of Prince Andrew's associations and legal troubles, as well as the departure of Prince Harry and Meghan Markle from their roles as senior royals. Despite these difficulties, she remained a unifying figure and a symbol of continuity for the nation.

Her Platinum Jubilee in 2022 marked an unprecedented milestone, celebrating 70 years on the throne. The celebrations highlighted her enduring popularity and the respect she commanded both at home and abroad. Her ability to adapt to changing times while maintaining the traditions of the monarchy was a testament to her skill as a leader and a figurehead.

Queen Elizabeth II's health began to decline in her final years, with the death of her beloved husband, Prince Philip, in 2021 marking a poignant moment in her later life. Despite these challenges, she continued to fulfill her duties, including appointing Liz Truss as prime minister just two days before her death.

Queen Elizabeth II passed away on September 8, 2022, at Balmoral Castle in Scotland. Her death marked the end of an era, and her legacy is characterized by her unwavering dedication to duty, her ability to adapt to a rapidly changing world, and her role as a stabilizing figure during times of significant national and global upheaval. Her life and reign left an indelible mark on the United Kingdom and the

Commonwealth, ensuring that her memory will endure for generations to come.

Epilogue

As we close the final chapter of "The Stories of Great Rulers," we are left with a profound sense of awe and reverence for the remarkable individuals whose lives and legacies we have explored. From the heights of power to the depths of adversity, they have shown us the extraordinary capabilities of human leadership and the enduring impact of their actions on the course of history.

Through the pages of this book, we have encountered rulers who rose to greatness through courage and determination, who navigated the turbulent currents of politics and war with skill and foresight, and who left an indelible mark on the world through their vision, ambition, and leadership.

But amidst the triumphs and glories of their reigns, we have also glimpsed the human side of these towering figures—their doubts and insecurities, their struggles and sacrifices, their moments of joy and sorrow. We have seen them grapple with the weight of responsibility, the burdens of power, and the complexities of ruling over diverse and often fractious societies.

And yet, through it all, they have persevered, driven by a sense of duty and devotion to their people and their realms. They have faced adversity with resilience and resolve, triumphed over adversity with courage and determination, and left behind a legacy that continues to inspire and captivate us to this day.

As we reflect on the lives and legacies of the Great Rulers, we are reminded of the timeless lessons they impart—the importance of leadership and statesmanship, the dangers of unchecked ambition and tyranny, and the enduring power of compassion, justice, and wisdom.

May their stories continue to resonate with us, inspiring us to strive for greatness in our own lives and to leave behind a legacy of service, integrity, and honor. And may we never forget the extraordinary individuals whose lives we have explored in these pages, for they have left an indelible mark on the tapestry of human history and the collective consciousness of mankind.

The End.